PRAISE FOR
POWER OF PROXIMITY

Great reminder: Who we are is who we associate with. Champions attract champions. Love this book!

Stephen Van Deventer
Founder of Asterion Cannabis, Inc.

We are a reflection of our peers. This book shares how to choose friends wisely.

Rob Angel, Founder, Pictionary

Our success is measured by the sphere of our influence. Change your circle—change your life.

General Marta Carcana

Hang around amazing people, and amazing things begin to happen.

Brian Smith, Founder, UGG

POWER *of*

proximity

DR. GREG REID

BONNIE FALLIN

SHANNON PARSONS

Power of Proximity

Dr. Greg Reid, Bonnie Fallin, with Shannon Parsons

Copyright ©2020

ISBN-13: 978-1-949001-10-5 print edition

Waterside Productions

Waterside Productions
2055 Oxford Ave
Cardiff, CA 92007
www.waterside.com

TABLE OF CONTENTS

FOREWORD

The people we know extend far beyond our immediate circle of family, friends, and coworkers. In fact, it has been documented that every person is only six degrees of separation from any other person. This means that it only takes six steps to connect any two people on the planet.

However, let's not forget that our world is connected more than ever before. With the popularity of the Internet and the ability to communicate via telephone, text, and email, the six steps have shortened. The beginning of the 21st century welcomed social media giants, including (in order of their introduction) LinkedIn, Facebook, YouTube, Twitter, WhatsApp, Instagram, Pinterest, and Snapchat. As a result of our ability to connect with others by simply following or friending another individual or group, the six degrees of separation shortened to just 3.5 in 2016. That number is expected to drop as social media users increase, and the gap will be closed the day everyone on the planet is virtually connected to everyone else.

Until that day, we can enjoy the fewest degrees of separation in history. Today, we already have access to the people who have the knowledge and experience we seek through the people we know and the connections we make, whether they are within our community or across the world. This is called the power of proximity.

What is the real power of proximity? In achieving success, it is the remarkable access to the greatest minds and experts of our time. It is the ability to reach out to someone we know and be connected to them and the people they know in record time. This is true regardless of your industry or the type of information you seek.

It has been said that nobody becomes successful alone. That has been true for centuries, and time has only supported that philosophy. As businesses expand on a global basis, the challenges businesses face expands, as well. As people become more knowledgeable, there is a need for more than information—there is a need to benefit from the wisdom and experience of those who have successfully overcome challenges and uncovered proven, timeless principles of success. We call these wise leaders and teachers "mentors."

With this book, you are just a few degrees of separation from the mentors who can change your life. In *The Power of Proximity*, you will meet some renowned experts and leaders who share their experience, insight, and wisdom, before introducing you to an expert who is within proximity to them.

Learn from them and then use the power of your own proximity to connect with the leaders and experts in your life … and the people they know … and the people they know. You get the idea.

Success is just a few degrees—and people—away. Close the gap with *The Power of Proximity*.

To your success,

Frank Shankwitz
Creator and Co-Founder, Make A Wish Foundation

CHAPTER ONE

MAKING CONNECTIONS

"How was your day?" It was the same question Meredith's mother asked her every evening when she arrived to pick up her son, Matthew. And her answer was usually the same—a nonchalant, unenthusiastic "fine."

Today was different, though. It was Friday, meaning her work week was over, but she suddenly realized that picking up her son was the best part of her day, as it should be. But what really stuck out was the fact that she couldn't say she had actually had a good day. Truth be told, by all accounts, she had accomplished little that day, or even that week.

Meredith was an insurance agent, and while there had been lean times, she had usually gotten through them. There was even a period when she was doing rather well and her sales were on a consistent rise. That was no longer true. She was lucky if she got one new client a week, and sometimes that was difficult. She wasn't alone, though. Her regional sales director and district manager were voicing their expectations, and everyone was feeling the pressure to perform at a higher level. It was frustrating. She'd tried everything and had given up on cold calls, which in the past were ineffective and a surefire way to stamp out any ambition or encouragement she might have had. And networking was nearly impossible. After all, she was a single parent of a four-year-old boy, and she felt she spent too little time with him as it was. It would be too difficult to add networking and social events to her already full plate. Besides, Matthew needed her and deserved her time and attention.

"My day was okay, Mom. I'm just glad this week is over, and I don't have to go to the office for a couple days," Meredith answered.

"I've always said you work too hard. Maybe it would be a good idea if you took a vacation," her mom replied.

"Now is definitely not a good time for that, Mom. Policies are down, even among existing clients. People want to do everything online now, and that leaves out the middleman— me. Maybe I've lost my touch. I don't know what the answer is, but something has to change," Meredith said.

"You're trying to do too much. You go to work and come straight home to take care of Matthew. You're a good mom, but maybe you need a break. Isn't there a workshop or conference or something you can attend? It might give you some ideas and reignite some of that fire you used to have," her mother suggested.

"The company always has seminars and stuff, Mom. But I'd have to leave Matthew overnight …"

"And he'll be fine here with me," her mom interrupted. "At least think about it. It might be good for you to get away. If things are as slow as you say, it couldn't hurt."

****

It was a couple weeks later when later when the opportunity came, and she almost overlooked it. She was thumbing through the mail that Charlotte, her assistant, had sorted and placed on her desk. Setting aside a few items she needed to tend to, she flipped through the rest, most of which was junk mail. But one item caught her eye, and it intrigued her. It was from Greg Reid, an author she followed on social media, who was holding a seminar. Turning it over, she read about the event and realized that she recognized some of the speakers' names. They were founders and CEOs of a variety of companies and industries, as well as a couple celebrities and the founder of one of the world's largest not for profits. It sounded so different and unique that she found herself hoping she could attend.

After checking her calendar to make sure she was free, Meredith visited the website printed on the flyer. She wavered back and forth for 15 minutes, halfheartedly trying to talk herself out of going. But she knew her mom was right. What she was doing wasn't working; she had to do *something*. Quickly, before she changed her mind, she registered for the event. If nothing else, it might do her some good to get away for a couple days. A change of scenery might change her perspective.

****

She was right. The weather in San Diego was gorgeous. She had never visited the city before, but it didn't disappoint. The downtown skyline was impressive, and the bay was breathtaking. Her Uber driver pointed out a few attractions on the way to the hotel and told her to make sure she visited the ocean during her stay. For the first time, she was really beginning to look forward to the next few days. It was certainly better than being in the office, she thought.

The next morning, she walked into the large conference room where the two-day seminar was being held. According to the materials she received, the first day would focus on "The Power of Proximity," and during the second day, the guest speakers would hold an open session, where they would interact with the attendees and provide them with advice based on their experiences. Finding a seat near the aisle, she pulled out her phone and checked in with Charlotte and her mom, pausing momentarily to nod and smile at the gentleman who sat next to her.

Right on time, the presenter, Greg Reid, took the stage. Not missing a beat, he dove straight into what he called "the power of proximity." He explained that he had based his career on helping others find and fulfill their purpose. Like a modern-day Napoleon Hill, he based his philosophies on the wisdom of the mentors he'd met and admired.

Meredith felt like he was talking directly to her when he said that everyone has the people they need to achieve success in their lives … directly or through other people they know. However, most people fail to let anyone know when they need advice or assistance, so those people are outside of their reach. Hearing that, Meredith silently admitted that she was guilty of avoiding other people and situations where she would be in proximity with others, especially after Matthew was born.

Then Greg stated exactly how Meredith felt—that traditional networking doesn't produce the results people want. One reason is that they are looking for instant gratification; they want results and they want them *now*. Unfortunately, they give up because they fail to see that it is a process—every connection can bring them closer to the connection that will change their careers and lives. Like dominos, one must fall before you can get to the last one.

Greg explained that this seminar would answer many questions, including one of the most universal of all time: what are they secrets to success? Not only would he and the other esteemed speakers divulge some of those secrets, but the seminar would bring everyone in the audience closer to people who could help them. They might be on the stage, they could be people sitting near them in the audience, or they could be someone that those people knew.

The seminar was packed with sessions and speakers, but the host kept the pace moving, and the content was so interesting that time flew quickly. When the day ended, Meredith was surprised. She actually could have listened for a few more hours and felt not only energized, but motivated. Everyone else must have felt the same way, because the crowd didn't disperse when the last speaker exited the stage. Instead, everyone mingled, happily sharing their insights and thoughts.

When they finally went their separate ways, Meredith returned to her hotel and was glad for the opportunity to soak in all she had learned, along with a few rays of the late afternoon sun.

She went over the day's events and speakers in her mind, recalling the nuggets of wisdom Greg and his panel had shared, along with their amazing journeys to success. She couldn't wait to hear what tomorrow would bring. But in the meantime, nature was bringing her one of the most glorious sunsets she had ever seen, and she intended to enjoy every minute of it.

***

The fresh air and new surroundings energized Meredith, and she was excited for the second day of the seminar. She sat in the same chair, but this time, she took the initiative to introduce herself to the gentleman next to her. Now was as good of a time as any to put what she'd learned into practice. Guessing him to be in his mid-50s, Meredith found him to be cordial and discovered that he had once been part of the information technology boom in Silicon Valley but had to make a career change after the dot.com crash. Now a small business owner, he told Meredith he was at the seminar to get some growth tips from the successful entrepreneurs on stage. As they talked, Meredith realized Greg was right—even though they had different careers and had taken different paths, they were similar in that they were both seeking a higher degree of success. It wasn't traditional networking, where everyone seems to always want to walk away with a prospect or new customer. However, she found she learned more about him in this environment than she would have elsewhere. There were no ulterior motives, just genuine interest and respect among two professionals.

Their conversation was interrupted when the microphone was turned on and Greg took the stage with the same high level of energy and enthusiasm he'd displayed the day before. Today, they'd be hearing from a new slate of speakers. Again, they were impressive on paper, but they were nothing short of remarkable on stage. They spoke directly and openly, sharing their successes, as well as their failures. Most of all, though, they openly shared real stories of struggles and opportunities and how one person or one key principle had a huge impact on their success.

Some were actors, and some were inventors. A professional athlete was among them, as well as the founder of a few companies and products that were household names across the world. They weren't all professional speakers, but they all contributed something unique to the audience.

As she listened intently, Meredith was surprised to realize that these people started out much like her—some were employed by others, while others struggled to find their niche and purpose. Some knew precisely what they wanted and set out with gusto to get it, while others struggled until they applied certain principles of success toward a new endeavor. They had several things in common, though—they were all living a life full of success and abundance and were committed to helping others benefit from their experience.

One particular woman caught Meredith's attention. A real estate professional, speaker, and author, Bonnie Fallin spoke about opportunities, something most people fail to recognize.

She pointed out that opportunities are in everything that happens, good and bad. Like the silver lining in a cloud, they're present in everything we do, but she said we fail to see them. However, they're there, often right in front of our face. Like she said, "Don't wait for opportunity to come knocking at your door and introduce itself. It won't. But it's there, waiting for you to notice it. It's so close, if it was a snake, it would have bit you." Before she exited the stage, Meredith jotted a quick note to remind herself to order Bonnie's book when she returned home.

Then, Greg took the stage once again. After thanking the panel of speakers and the audience for making the event a resounding success, he left them with some parting words.

"In the last two days, you've met some amazing people with some incredible stories. They are all champions. You are a champion, too. You can do everything they have done and be the master of your own success. But you can't do it alone. Nobody can. Thankfully, you have my secret weapon, which is the power of proximity. Everyone in this room and everyone they know are now within your circle. Connect with them, and learn from them. It's the best way to fast track the road to success and happiness. But when you arrive at your destination, don't forget that the greatest benefit you will receive is your ability to help others succeed. Pass on your experience and wisdom to the people you meet. Like I've always said, the greatest gift you'll ever know is helping others learn and grow."

CHAPTER TWO

EVERYTHING WE NEED IS
ALREADY AROUND US

Meredith hoped the two-hour flight home would give her an opportunity to discover what path to take—just what was her purpose and identity? At one time, she thought she knew the answer to that question, but things had changed. As a mother, her identity and priorities had shifted. Her happiness wasn't the only thing at stake, and she had responsibilities that made her reluctant to take risks. But she realized that it was for that reason that it was even more important for her to focus on her career.

Before she had a real opportunity to dwell on it, a woman sat in the seat next to her. Meredith didn't know her name, but she recognized her face—she had seen her several times at the seminar.

"Hi, I believe I just saw you at Greg Reid's seminar, didn't I?" she asked.

"Yes, you did! I've attended several of his events over the past few years. I learn something new every time," she said.

"You've been to several of his events? This was my first one, but I really enjoyed it. I'm sorry we didn't have a chance to talk then, but I'm glad to run into you now. My name is Meredith Grant."

"It's good to meet you, Meredith. I'm Michele Malo. It's nice to sit next to someone who also went to the event. I'm usually so inspired and motivated after these seminars that it helps to talk about it with other people."

"What do you do, Michele?"

"To give you the short elevator speech, I'm a coach, consultant, and an author. Greg and I have mutual friends in our circle, and he has played a role in my success, as well. Now, tell me about yourself, Meredith," invited Michele.

Meredith replied, providing Michele with an abbreviated version of her resume.

When Michele asked her what brought her to the retreat, Meredith explained that her growth, as well as her enthusiasm, had stalled, and she had hoped the retreat would bring her some inspiration or insight to put a spark back into both.

"Did it?" Michele asked.

"Yes, oh yes, but it also invited more questions. Greg and the other speakers really gave me some tools that I'm sure will improve my marketing results, and I'm grateful for that. But

I've come to realize that I'm not as happy with my career as I once was," Meredith admitted.

"Meredith, let me tell you about myself. I once weighed 300 pounds and was one of the sickest 28-year-old women you'd ever meet. Literally. I mean, I called in fat to work," she chuckled. "Then I figured out what was weighing me down. So let me ask you, Meredith, what's weighing you down?"

"I've lost some of the passion for what I do, and I'm not sure if I can get that back, or if I even want to. But I have a little boy, so it's probably not a good time to make a major career change," Meredith answered.

"Whatever is wrong, I want you to know that you can fix it— one connection at a time, one decision at a time. I made a career change once, so I know what you're going through. I went through the journey of leaving corporate America and putting myself out there in unchartered waters. I've been through weight loss and divorce, but I've also met some amazing people. What I've found is that there are people who will help you accomplish whatever you want to do. Don't talk yourself out of your goals—instead, find the right people to help you reach them," Michele advised.

"I just don't know who those people are," Meredith replied.

"Well, what you don't think is a connection at the time can be the most important thing you need in that moment. It's give and take. You just have to ask yourself what you can do to enhance others and what they can do to enhance you. But you have to get out there and be present. Nothing happens when you are sitting in your living room."

"Now, I know you have a child, but that shouldn't deter you from doing what makes you happy. Quite the contrary, your happiness is important to your child," Michele stated. "You have to have a life and expand your horizons. It doesn't matter what you decide to do or what industry you're in, you absolutely will need to engage with others. I've learned when I don't do that, that's when things go south."

"You're right. I just wish I could know what I want. It would sure make it easier," Meredith responded.

"Of course, it would. But our growth is a journey, and sometimes the lessons and answers take time. That's when you need to re-engage and find a mentor, someone you respect who cares about you. That's what I did. At first, I thought it wouldn't be easy to find the right people, but what I discovered is that everything we need is already around us," Michele said.

"If I decide to do something different and change careers, I'd have to admit that I'm a failure at what I do. I guess I'm not good with change," Meredith admitted.

"Change does not mean failure. If you've made mistakes or find that you need to make a life or career change, there will be times when moving forward feels like you're leaving something behind. And that's okay. Give yourself permission to grieve and a moment to ground yourself. At that time, you're not in a good place to make major decisions. But, and this is important, don't stay there long. I suggest you use that moment to gain clarity to move forward, and then ask for counsel to get to a better place. It won't always be easy—there will be moments when the wind gets knocked out of you; take a moment to breathe and get back into the game when that happens. I know—I was married for 21 years and then got divorced. I had to take some time and space to get my confidence back in order to do the things I knew I was capable of," Michele told her.

"Wow, 21 years is a long time," remarked Meredith.

"Yes, it is. So you can see that I've had major changes in my life—a divorce, a significant weight loss, and a career change. And I'm here to tell you that you can do it, too. It might not be easy, but you'll find it was worth it," said Michele.

"Wow, Michele, I sat down on this plane and didn't know you at all. Strange, isn't it, that I was sitting next to the one person who not only understands what I'm going through, but who has the experience and wisdom to offer their advice?"

"It's not that strange, Meredith. Remember, the people we need are already around us, and I'm not the exception. And one of the reasons I am able to offer you the advice you need at this moment is that I listen very intently. Everyone needs something so very different. I offered you the advice that I felt was best suited for you right now," Michele said.

"And I appreciate it. I really I do. I just hope I can apply it."

Grabbing a piece of paper from her purse, Michele jotted down her phone number and email address. Handing it to Meredith, she said, "Here you go. I invite you to contact me whenever you have a question or you're experiencing doubt. I want to help. I'm a coach and connector, and I want to support you."

"Thank you. But I'm not so sure I can reciprocate. How can I enhance you?" Meredith inquired.

"Discovering that is part of the process. I have faith that we are all here to help each other and that we were meant to connect. Like I said, the people we need are already around us, but we have to connect with them to discover why," Michele explained.

"I'm glad we connected, Michele."

"So am I. As I've been known to say, you never know the one person who can change the trajectory of your life, but I do know that it is my goal to make a positive change in the lives of everyone I meet. If you need anything, don't hesitate to let me know. If I can't help you, I probably know someone who can. That's why they call me a connector," Michele said.

"You're awesome, Michele. I hope I can take you up on that offer!"

CHAPTER THREE

THE HERO'S JOURNEY

After tucking Matthew in and reading him his favorite book, she put him to bed before opening her laptop and checking to see if she had any correspondence that needed to be addressed before Monday morning. Finding only a few inquiries from potential clients or meeting requests, Meredith sighed and told herself that she had to find a way to turn this around.

Meredith's mind went back to what she'd learned in the seminar and her talk with Michele on the flight home. Always considerate, she understood the importance of following up with people, so she took a moment to send Michele Malo an email, thanking her for taking the time to listen to her and offer advice. To her surprise, Michele responded right away, telling her that she was happy to meet and know her. She also suggested that she thought Meredith would benefit from having a coach to guide her on her journey of self-discovery and improvement. Taking it one step further, Michele sent her an introduction to Shannon Parsons, who she called a friend and a superhero, and encouraged them to connect. "Shannon can help you see everything from a fresh perspective. I'm sure you'll benefit from knowing her."

Excited, Meredith immediately contacted Shannon, providing her with her contact information and telling her she looked forward to talking to her when it was convenient. The next day, Shannon replied, and they scheduled a phone call for Sunday morning.

Meredith immediately discovered that Michele was right— after listening to Meredith describe her current issues, Shannon pointed out one of the problems many women face in overcoming challenges, which was that they have difficulty facing them without expressing their problems. Being stuck in the pain of their past, they cannot move forward and gain resiliency. This "woe is me" tendency keeps women from benefitting from their empowerment.

"Shannon, I confess I'm guilty of that, too. I always tell people that I'm a single mother, and it usually leads to a conversation about how difficult it is to be a single parent with a full-time job," Meredith confessed.

"It happens with everyone, actually," Shannon replied. "People tend to identify and connect through their shared problems. Too often, though, we don't even realize we're doing it."

"You are right. Often, the conversation takes the same path, and before anyone knows it, we're all talking about how busy we all are. Maybe I am falling back on that as an excuse. But I have to confess, I have no idea what my empowerment is, so I don't think I can benefit from it," Meredith said.

"Trust me, you are empowered, and there is a way to discover that empowerment, Meredith. I've devised a three-step system based on what is commonly known as The Hero's Journey, specifically for that purpose. Each step starts with an 'I', and it's rather easy to follow. The first step is Introspection. This is where you look into the past and your struggles and how you overcame them. What did you have to do to get through the hardship? Then, identify what kind of internal power you had to tap into to be able to overcome that hardship. That internal power made you better, stronger, or more resilient. You might not see it right away, but believe me, it's there. The second 'I' is Integration. How is that circumstance or challenge part of you today? For instance, if you grew up in a family that struggled financially, you might be particularly keen about your finances. Maybe you're great with a budget or you save a percentage of your income every week without fail. Then, the third 'I' is Implementation. How are you going to take this superhero part of you and use it for good in your everyday world? It's also important to ask yourself how you are going to use your newly-discovered superhero power to help others," Shannon explained.

"No matter what your challenges or difficulties are, Meredith, if you are alive, you are stronger and more resilient than you were before those things happened. Dig deep and discover the benefits you gained from going through those situations or circumstances, and you'll discover your strength."

"Wow. You know, you're right! When I think about it, I can see that I'm capable of so much more than I ever thought I'd be. Five years ago, I would have never imagined that I could raise a little boy by myself. Back then, I struggled to accomplish the things I needed to do, and I would have never believed that I could take on more, especially something as time consuming as parenthood!" Meredith replied.

"So, you've gotten better at time management. You might be more flexible than you used to be; maybe you're now a pro at setting priorities or boundaries in your life. Everything in life happens for a reason, Meredith. There are no coincidences. And if you use your experiences to grow, you'll find that you are better because of it. You're stronger. When you're aware of that, you can leave your woes behind and put on a superhero cape and take advantage of the incredible power and lessons those woes taught you," Shannon said.

"I get it! It's like what doesn't kill me makes me stronger, right?" Meredith asked.

"Exactly. Things will always happen in our lives that set us back or pose challenges. We can get stuck in the 'why me' mode, or we can look for the silver lining and use it to line our cape and declare to the world that we are better for it," Shannon explained.

"You are so awesome. Just talking to you makes me feel like I can conquer the world! I know I can take your hero's journey, Shannon. I'm just not sure where I want that journey to take me. Do I use it to try to rebuild my career, or should I explore other possibilities? I wish I had the answers," Meredith sighed.

"We all do. The point is to avoid staying stuck in your journey without harnessing the gifts that the journey brings you along the way, regardless which path you choose," Shannon advised. "We all tend to tell ourselves stories, but they are rarely in the place of triumph in adversity. But Meredith, we are actually meant to go through adversity so we can find that gift, that growth, and the triumph that comes from it. Trust me, CEOs know this, and they know the value that can be gained from the experience. The coolest thing is that when you become aware of that value for yourself, it is cleansing, and it draws people to you. People actually are attracted to positive energy, not negative energy, and this helps you develop relationships and opportunities."

"That's incredible, Shannon!"

"What's more incredible is that you can apply this three-step system, this journey, if you will, to any area of your life. I intentionally made the system so easy that anyone can do it. I've met a lot of people, though, who are really stuck in their struggles. If that happens to you, I advise you to stop whatever it is you are doing and create some type of brain break or a pattern disruption and intentionally get in the mode of feeling happy. Here's why—if you're working on a project or a goal, and you're not feeling happy or inspired, the energy you're feeling will come out into your project. The Internet might be slow or freeze. You might encounter random obstacles that keep you from progressing. When that happens, jump out of your chair, turn on some upbeat music, do whatever it takes to get energized and feel happy. When you do, you'll find that things start to go smoother and begin to work for you, rather than against you," Shannon added.

"You're right. It's like when one thing goes wrong, everything tends to go wrong," Meredith said.

"It's not just a belief, Meredith. There is science behind this philosophy, and I know it works because I teach it to at-risk youth and see the results all the time. You can't find solutions when your brain is in a stress response, but when you feel good, your energy will be elevated and your brain will be able to find the solutions you're looking for. It sounds easy, and it is, and it really does work. Try it. I believe you'll find the answers to what's weighing on your mind if you can find that positive place, where your brain will automatically come up with the answers you're looking for."

"I'd love for that to happen," Meredith replied.

"It will. You'll begin to see opportunities you didn't see before, and the people you need to make it them happen will come into your life. You might not even know them, but they will appear," Shannon said.

"I think they already are, Shannon. It's strange, but I've been meeting people like you and Michele since I went to Greg's seminar!"

"There are no coincidences. It's called the power of proximity. Every person you meet has the power to benefit you. The real question is, how are you going to use this to your advantage?" Shannon asked. "You are the only person who can answer that question. Just don't forget to look for the benefits around you — whether they are in your struggles or in the people you meet.

"Remember, you don't need to know how to do everything yourself, especially when it comes to making a major change in your life. You just need to know who to ask. May I suggest a good friend who can help?" Shannon asked.

"Can you?! Absolutely!" Meredith answered.

"Her name is Krystylle Richardson, and I think you'll find that she's fascinating. She's a very gracious and giving person. I'm sure she can offer you some help or insights," said Shannon.

"I'd appreciate that," Meredith said. "Thank you."

"You're welcome. But don't lose sight of the fact that the reason you are able to connect with people like Krystylle and others who might not have been available to you before is because of the power of proximity. With the people you meet, you get the benefits of the alliances they have made along the way," Shannon added. "They can help you unlock your strengths so you can discover your true powers."

CHAPTER FOUR

THE 7 L'S OF SUCCESS

True to her word, Shannon did contact her friend, asking her to reach out to Meredith. Krystylle Richardson had been a trusted friend for several years, and she had helped many of Shannon's clients. At the bottom of a mutual introduction email, Shannon said, "Krystylle, I've encouraged Meredith to connect with you when she's ready. I'm sure you two will benefit from knowing each other. Have a great day!"

Meredith waited to contact Krystylle; she wanted to have a clearer vision of what she wanted to do before they spoke. During the next week, she contemplated her future in her company. At the moment, there weren't any signs that business would be picking up in the immediate future. However, she knew she could make small gains if she put her mind to it. Being honest with herself, she admitted that she hadn't been diligent in procuring sales, making her partially responsible for her situation. If something else came along in the meantime, that would be great. But for now, she committed herself to putting extra effort into her job as an insurance agent. Going back to the basics, she poured herself into finding clients and increasing her sales.

Within a week, she had scheduled appointments with two new leads, a promising sign that she could succeed in the business until the day she knew what it was she really wanted to do with her career.

When the week drew to a close, Meredith reached out to Krystylle Richardson via her website. Expecting an automated response initially, she was surprised when Krystylle personally responded the next morning, suggesting they schedule a 30-minute "How May I Help" call so she could hear from Meredith and explain what she does and how it might be of benefit. Krystylle concluded her message with a Zoom call invitation for the next day.

Once on the call, Krystylle wasted no time and immediately introduced herself and told Meredith about herself.

"Hey Meredith," Krystylle said with a smile. "I am so happy to meet you and am glad we get a chance to share for a few moments and determine how I might be able to help." Krystylle explained. Krystylle then asked Meredith about herself and took a few notes while she spoke. When Meredith was done, Krystylle proceeded to share a bit about what she does. "I have been categorized as a transformational mindset life coach with an emphasis on leadership. I have a great passion for people and helping them to become the best version of themselves by giving them the tools to reproduce the process over and over again. Some corporate and individual clients have even called me a leadership expert, brilliant, and other words that I appreciate but don't consider as important. I want to do whatever I can to help you be a better you. One exercise I take people through, Meredith, is the use of what I call the 3E's. **Evaluate** the mind-trash that might be holding you back, help you to **Evict** your limiting beliefs, and then **Elevate** your thinking to lead a fearless, gratifying life full of purpose, power, passion, and profit. All of this helps you to ignite your uniqueness and then become the most impactful leader in your given area of expertise," she said.

"Oh well, maybe I'm not a suitable client then. You see, I don't categorize myself as a leader," Meredith admitted.

"I assure you that you are. My programs are focused on mindset, and especially that portion of the mindset related to leadership, because we are all leaders of something. We all have what I call "the leader within." We lead ourselves and our families. We are leaders of small businesses and corporations. We are even leaders of a line at a grocery store or a bank. Somewhere in our lives, we are leaders, even if we aren't aware of it," she replied.

"I hadn't thought of that. Okay, in what ways do you ignite the mindset?" Meredith inquired.

"After we go through some mindset exercises and a discovery session regarding your thoughts, I do an assessment using some proprietary techniques I've developed that are tailored to each person's situation and goals. Clients love this and sometimes discover things about themselves that they never realized. It's a kind of self-realization and an ah-ha moment for them most times. It is a pretty cool thing to see. We couple this with mindfulness, breathing techniques and more. Some other parts of the assessment are patterned after other more well-known leadership principles. The purpose is to get to your dreams and discover your mindset. Then, we figure out how that can be used to get you to your destiny. This encompasses exercises and questions, as well as mapping out your past and present and how it relates to your future. Sometimes, Meredith, what people think is their dream to destiny turns out to be different, and they discover it's something else altogether," explained Krystylle.

"Oh, this is something I know I need. So how do we proceed?" Meredith asked.

"I would tell you that one of the first things I suggest that you to do is close your eyes and think about nothing, nothing at all. Now, I know sometimes just saying that causes you to think about something, right? After all, our minds aren't used to not thinking. So I suggest that you try to empty your mind using the techniques mentioned earlier that I will teach you so we can look at your life and the things that brought you to this point." Krystylle stated.

"What happens then?" Meredith asked.

"Well, what happens is my favorite part; I might say that about all of the parts, though." Krystylle chuckled. "This is when we start the Eviction process and Elevation. When your mind is a clean slate, we can then use one of my other many tools to do what I call a Word Trio Assessment. We explore the words that present themselves. For instance, this technique has more parts to it, but one thing we do is a three-word exercise. This method is only used for discovery, depending on some factors related to what we find when we go through your discovery phase. For example, a word can be related to an emotion or a person, place, or thing. Let me explain further. Here we look at the word that pops into your mind, let's say that it was the word 'home.' Then we go through the analysis related to that word, and from there, we move on to the next word. Then the next word is assessed until we've covered all three words," Krystylle advised.

"The purpose of this exercise is to get a good look into your mindset, feelings, emotions, and other things as part of my proprietary and tailored method. Once we're done, we delve into the other areas that make sense based on your needs, including where you stand on your leadership aspirations."

"How does that work, Krystylle?" Meredith asked.

"Well, depending on what you are looking to do in your business, we outline an assessment report and plan to help you get there. We look at strengths and opportunities for improvement. I also like to look at what people feel they are good at, what makes them happy, and what is their why. We also include what might actually stretch them. This is a big one, and there is a special stretch exercise that I do for this portion of our time together. Stretching is key; do you agree? Or a better question might be, what do you feel stretching is?"

"Something that helps you grow, right?" Meredith added.

"Exactly, you got it. It helps us grow, as well as to identify some of the things that are holding us back. For instance, I was a victim of bullying throughout my school years and, at times, as an adult. Until I realized the emotions tied to those experiences were responsible for some of my hang ups, I couldn't break free from it. This analysis will help you identify issues like that in your life, and possibly lots of other things, as well," Krystylle shared.

Krystylle explained that there are 11 controversial lessons of strategies, leadership, and success and told Meredith she would send her a diagram that would help her see how they work together. Then she went on to explain a few of those lessons.

"Meredith, I call this 'Krystylle's 7 L's of Success. I will take you through just a brief description of a few of them, and the rest we can discuss when you have your sessions with me if you choose to move forward with the BEST VERSION OF ME coaching sessions or the DISCOVERING THE LEADER WITHIN sessions.

"Just looking at a few of the L's of success, not in any order, I will start with the L for Limber. You have to be flexible and open to other ideas and possibilities. But when you make up your mind, be clear, be decisive, and be the strength you want to see in your leaders.

"Another one of the L's of success is Leverage. Always cultivate the skills of your team and utilize them and your business tools to stay competitive and innovative.

"The third one I would look at for this brief review would be the L of Litmus. This means to always use a Litmus test. These are methods to measure your progress and success, methods that will test one hypothesis or choice versus another. This starts the process you need for brainstorming.

"Have joy and have fun in anything and everything you do. Be serious when necessary but not overly so no one wants to work with you, be around you, invest in you and so on. Laughter breeds fulfillment in your life, do your darndest to create a productive, but fun and creative atmosphere at work, home, and everywhere.

"Wow, Krystylle. That was a lot! I see why your clients value your coaching so much; you are very thorough in what you do. All of the upfront analysis and the few of the 7 L's of Success you mentioned seem like they would help me. Some seem involved, and others seem like they'd be easy to implement. I can already see where I'm lacking in some of those L's," Meredith commented.

"Not only are they applicable in all areas of life, Meredith, but they're effective. As long as you stay true to them, you'll progress," Krystylle added.

"I wish I'd heard of your 7 L's before! Is there anything else I need to know?"

"Well, yes, but I don't want your head to explode." They both laughed. "Your success toolkit is very important. My goal for each client is to only put in it what you specifically need based on you. Some coaches try to force fit all tools on all clients, but that is not how I roll. I take the time to really listen and create your toolkit contents based on foundational principles. I personally was tired of the roller coaster of my emotions and had to do something about it. I was tired of my thoughts of failure and fear and had to make some intentional SHIFTS in my mindset and my life. You seem to have some of those same thoughts rolling around in your head because I see your head nodding, am I right?"

Meredith once again nodded her head in agreement.

"Well, that's about it for the time we have for our call. I think we went a little over, but that is okay. I really feel we would work well together, and I am looking forward to hearing more about your journey, hopes, and dreams, PLUS your challenges and fears. I love to squash those." Krystylle smiled, and so did Meredith. "Just never forget that God created us all unique so we will be able to change the world with power, purpose, and the use of our live-out-loud passion. You do have power and purpose; we all do. Trust me, you will find it," Krystylle remarked.

"I sure hope so. I want to have more passion about my life, as well. You sure helped me to see that I need that," Meredith replied.

"You will. Until then, no matter what happens, don't be afraid to find yourself and surely don't be afraid to be yourself. To be yourself, you need to know who you are. Using the tools we discussed and filling up that toolkit is certain to get you there in no time" Krystylle added. Meredith put up her hand to high-five Krystylle, and she accepted. Meredith seemed pumped about the session and told Krystylle she would definitely think about all that was shared, thanked her, and commented that she would definitely be in touch.

CHAPTER FIVE

THE MINDSET OF GROWTH

Meredith wasted no time thanking Shannon for introducing her to Krystylle.

"Wow! She spent so much time with me. Actually, it seemed like she covered a lot of territory, but Krystylle has so much to offer and her sessions are so in depth that I'm sure I'm going to be talking to her much more. Thanks, Shannon, for the introduction," Meredith said.

"I'm glad to help. Hey, a good friend of mine is going to be out your way on Friday. His name is David Chametzky, and he has a lot of experience helping people conquer their fears. He usually fills the house, but if you think you might be able to get away for the afternoon, I'll give him a call and see if they can squeeze one more person in," Shannon offered.

"I'll make sure I can get away! I'd love to attend! Let me know what you hear, okay?"

"Sure thing. I'll get back with you as soon as I know something," Shannon promised.

The next morning, Shannon sent her a text message: Hey, check your email. I sent you a guest pass to David's event. Just print it out and take it with you. Have fun!

***

Meredith walked into the convention room the next Friday and noticed that, although the room was full, it was an event similar to the seminar she'd attended in San Diego. While the room buzzed as groups engaged in muffled conversations, Meredith presented her guest pass and grabbed the program for the afternoon.

Once she found a seat, she perused the program for David Chametzky's name, finding that he was the opening speaker on the agenda. His bio stated he was a mentor and coach who worked with international businesses, corporations, and individuals, helping them find their best self and personal attitudes toward happiness.

When David took the stage, the words he spoke were directly related to Meredith's situation.

After sharing his experience, David introduced the audience to what he called the Phoenix Paradigm Shift.

"The Phoenix Paradigm Shift is a mindset of growth. It utilizes the many stories around the story of the mythical Phoenix, the mythical bird who lives its life, then dies and turns to ashes. It is then reborn and reemerges out of its own ashes to begin anew. The same holds true with us. We have the capability at any given time to be reborn and reemerge stronger, brighter, and better than before, finding the ways within ourselves to ignite the fire in our belly to lift ourselves from the ashes of previous challenges and opportunities of growth," he explained.

"We've probably all had life experiences that held negative pieces within us, leaving us to believe we cannot possibly do this anymore. We're exhausted, frightened, and discouraged. To us, this moment in time marks the end of everything that was important to us. Somehow, though, we manage to go on. Looking back, we can see that we faced challenges, but we didn't die an eternal death. Somehow, we picked ourselves up and reemerged, and our life hadn't ended. It had gotten better! In the future, we can look back and see how things changed and what we learned from those negative experiences. We find we didn't give up, but we were reborn. We are Phoenixes," David said.

"Most of us are no strangers to challenges. I like to use the wisdoms of the ages and metaphors to assist others to see their Phoenix moment. One of the many gems of wisdom I enjoy using is something Winston Churchill once said: if you're going through hell, keep going. The idea is if you're going through something overwhelming, don't quit and try to run from it. Instead, figure out a way to get through it and conquer it once and for all. That's your Phoenix moment, where the Phoenix Paradigm Shift occurs.

"My Phoenix moment came about 15 years ago. I was getting a divorce and thought my life was over. Obviously, it was not. In fact, I'm actually living my best life right now. At the time, though, I didn't know how I was going to get through the next day, let alone the rest of my life.

"What did I do? I broke it down as small as possible. Instead of getting through it one hour or day at a time, I focused on getting through ten minutes at a time. Chunk it down to five minutes if you have to. When you see each challenge as a moment in time instead of a moment that marks time, you can put it in perspective, and you can get through some of your greatest challenges. I know it works. I've worked with people suffering from various stresses, life's battles, and challenges. They can be so traumatized that they sometimes freeze up and are literally unable to do anything. When that happens, I tell them to focus on the now, nothing else, just the present moment. When they do that, it seems to reframe them, and they can then focus on the next ten minutes and then the next. Eventually, they find they were able to get through that all-consuming moment and come out a little stronger and more in control.

"Obviously, you don't have to have extreme stress or anxiety to apply this technique. But we are all warriors of some type, and everyone has won battles no one else might know or understand. I have not personally fought in a war, but I've been a life warrior. I've worked with people who have suffered from addiction and found recovery. They, too, are warriors. They fought battles that people don't understand. There are many types of battles, and you might have your own. If so, you are a life warrior, too, and you can apply this strategy to your Phoenix moment."

David then shared the best way to address fear, which holds people back from many opportunities.

"I mentored a young woman who had a very real fear of flying. Just thinking about or passing an airport caused her to have a panic attack. She was only 20 years old, and she came to me because she was supposed to go on a birthright trip to Israel with her college friends, but she didn't think there was any way she could do it. The trip was already scheduled, and we didn't have much time to help her overcome her fear. But I work in an accelerated way, and we got through a lot of trauma quickly and were able to move forward. In the end, she got on that plane and had one of the greatest trips of her life. As a result, she said the world opened up to her. On the other side of your fear lies your opportunities.

"But her experience wasn't without challenges. She made it through the flight there, but when they landed, her luggage was lost. Bordering on panic, she called me and frantically asked me what she should do. I calmly replied, 'So you get to go shopping! Have fun!' Just like that, a switch turned off and she stopped panicking and saw the situation in a positive light.

"She was looking at the situation as a problem, instead of an opportunity. That is one of the benefits of stepping away and getting through the moment, one step at a time. She happily flies everywhere now, where she was once limited to only experience places and things that were within driving distance.

"You, too, can overcome fear," he said. "The key is to find a way to get through whatever frightens you just once. The first time is the hardest. After that, it gets easier and easier every time. With every new experience, you grow legs, and your legs get stronger over time."

David then applied his principles to his work with corporate executives.

"The Phoenix Paradigm promotes growth in all areas. It's not only applicable to an individual situation. I've worked with corporations, too, and I have walked into boardrooms. The first time I walked into a boardroom was a scary experience. I was out of my comfort zone. But now I know I can do this, and I no longer have any fear when I'm asked to. It also might surprise some to realize that executives also experience fear—they appear to be confident and assured most of the time, but they also experience situations that pose challenges, and sometimes they are overwhelmed. Sometimes, they make mistakes. I remind them that they have a Phoenix mindset. It is built within us all, and we just need to find a way to tap back into it. They can turn any negative experience into an opportunity and reinvent themselves. They can come out of this experience even stronger. It's an evolutionary process of growth, and that growth is what will take you to your destination."

David was truly inspirational, and his words caused Meredith to think about her fears and how she could turn them into opportunities. She didn't know what those opportunities were just yet, but David had taught her that she could get through it, one moment, one hour, one day at a time.

At the end of the afternoon, the speakers moved among groups and continued to share their expertise. The advice was abundant, and the insight was enlightening, even fun!

Meredith didn't even feel uncomfortable sharing when David approached and personally introduced himself. He opened the conversation up and asked them to each share their fears. With every answer, he offered a solution, proving that when you aren't focused entirely on the problem, you are able to recognize the opportunities. It was an effective way for him to demonstrate the real application of the Phoenix Mindset and show them that it works in every situation.

When it was her turn, Meredith shared her fear that a career change might be necessary, but it came with a huge risk. What if it didn't work? What if she failed? How would she support her son?

David listened patiently to every word, and then responded.

"This is your Phoenix moment—it's your opportunity to pause and move past your fear, one moment at a time. Then look for the positive in the negative—inside your current experience is an opportunity. Begin to look for the solution and stop focusing on the problem. Meredith, that is when you will find your rebirth. That is when you'll experience growth," he said.

CHAPTER SIX

PLANNING FOR SUCCESS

On Monday morning, Meredith dove right into her work. She focused on integrating Krystylle Richardson's 7 L's of success into her business and took David Chametzky's advice and started looking for solutions, instead of dwelling on the problems. Knowing it would give her a competitive advantage, she spent a considerable amount of time personalizing and enhancing the benefits she offered her clients, such as comparing policies to offer the best coverage at the lowest cost and providing transparency by disclosing how she is compensated.

Late that afternoon, she received an email from David Chametzky, thanking her for attending his event and apologizing that there hadn't been enough time for him to speak longer with her.

In Meredith's reply, she told him how much she had enjoyed his speech and that it had really resonated with her current situation.

He welcomed Meredith to contact him if he could be of assistance in finding her personal attitude toward happiness, then offered to connect her with an individual who he felt would benefit her on a professional level.

"Johanna Godinez is a leader in the business arena. She is a human success development coach, who will help you define your idea of success, understand your potential, and assist you in creating a plan of action. She will help you understand how to develop, integrate and revise a successful plan of action. Although she focuses mainly on businessmen changing careers or planning life after retirement, I am certain that she can use her methods to help facilitate your progress. I will send you both a mutual introductory email, and you two can take it from there."

"Thank you, David. I look forward to connecting with her," Meredith replied.

By the time Meredith opened her messages, Johanna had already written back. She planned to be holding a corporate event in the area in the following week and could meet Meredith for lunch before her return flight, if she was available. After firming the arrangements, Johanna encouraged Meredith to visit her website and learn more about her coaching style.

On Johanna's website, Meredith learned about her business, Life and Style Coaches. As a human success development coach and entrepreneur with a Master's in Business

Administration, Johanna had received high praise from her clients for helping them in not only their businesses, but also their personal lives and even their image by working on their sense of style. Johanna's passion and inspiration were evident, her positive and encouraging words, clips on the news, and articles published in her blog helped Meredith feel connected to her. She related right away to one particular article Johanna had published, entitled "Starting a New Business Venture," in which discussed how to plan for a successful business endeavor and addressed the best way to respond to any fear that might arise during a career transition. It was as if she'd written the article specifically for her.

Not knowing what to expect, Meredith was feeling a bit anxious. However, when they met, Johanna immediately put her at ease, describing her coaching business and services in a friendly and easy-to-understand manner.

"I trust David gave you a brief background about me, but let me tell you a little about myself. Typically, I work with the corporate sector, and most of my clients are men that are approaching retirement or going through a mid-life epiphany that is urging them to make changes in their lives. In a nut shell, I help people break down the various aspects that encompass health and affect their lives, including their internal health, which includes physical, psychological, emotional, and spiritual factors; and their external health, which includes relationships, environmental, career, and financial health. The tools that I apply can provide you with some advice, food for thought, and guidance that will be beneficial during this transition time. As we begin to uncover where your life does not support your career change, we can begin to create actions that will keep you in alignment by incorporating strategies into your life that can help you create the clarity of mind needed to manifest what you desire," Johanna explained.

"That is exactly what I need! I really appreciate you taking the time to meet with me today, Johanna."

"You may not be in the target market I focus on, but I have worked with individuals in all walks of life and if David trusts that you could benefit from my services, I'm happy to help in any way I can. I understand just how important it is to have someone to turn to for trusted advice. Because I want to make sure I provide you with the level and type of coaching that will benefit you the most, I strive to learn as much about you as possible. In that way, we can be assured that you will receive coaching in the areas that will benefit you the most."

"Absolutely, I guess it is easier to make a change when you know where to start," Meredith stated

"Here is a basic overview of how Life and Style Coaches works. There are eight areas of our life that affect the state of our health. By mapping those eight areas, we can gauge where in your life you could make shifts to create alignment and balance. For example, there might be a relationship that is preventing you from moving forward from the past, or there may be habits in your personal life that unknowingly are holding you back from making progress. When we have scenarios consistently rolling over in our minds, they create a sort of hamster wheel in our thoughts. As they constantly turn and replay themselves over and over, you fail to realize how much these thoughts patterns are affecting you. That being said, can you pinpoint anything right off the bat that you feel is holding you back in the process of your growth, Meredith?"

"I feel like my career is causing my life to become stagnant. My sales numbers have been steadily declining, and I am not motivated to work harder. In fact, I've even considered leaving the insurance industry altogether. I'm reluctant to make major changes in my life. I don't really have another career in mind and having the sole responsibility for my son and his needs means that I must make responsible choices for the both of us. What if I try something else and regret it later? Or much worse... what if I fail?" Meredith asked.

"The fear of failure can be paralyzing, but it isn't uncommon. Fear, however, is not the real issue—the real question you need to answer is, where is that fear coming from? Is it because you're not prepared financially, emotionally, or mentally? Do you lack the confidence to successfully make a career change, or do you fear change itself? You must determine the causes of your fears so you can address them accordingly and prepare yourself as much as possible for the failures that are sure to come. Yes, you heard that right, Meredith. You have to give yourself permission to fail, because you will fail a few times. It is inevitable. No matter how great your plan is, there will be times when things do not work the way you would like them to. Be aware of your potential stumbling blocks beforehand, so you have a plan in place in the event they should arise. For example, in 2016, I left my life and work to volunteer for six months with endangered sea turtles in Costa Rica. A trip of that magnitude involved a lot of preparation, not only financially, but mentally and in my career. After all, when I returned, I still needed to have a job and a place to live. Leaving my life and work for six months was a risk, but I found that proper planning was a great way to minimize the risks," Johanna advised.

"So, I need to have a plan in place in case I fail?" Meredith asked.

"Yes; there are also other reasons why it is important to have a plan in place. You will need to have sufficient funds to support your family and provide for their needs. There might be obstacles or issues that delay your progress, and you wouldn't want that to be the reason why you don't succeed. The point is, you can't foresee what might happen, so it is important for you to prepare for all possible setbacks," Johanna answered.

"That makes sense. It's both logical and responsible," Meredith said.

"Exactly! Having enough money to support yourself during a career transition is important. But you don't need a six-figure bank account to take steps toward what you want. While you're making a career shift, you have other options. For instance, you might want to stay where you are, on a part-time basis while you start building your business up, or you might need to create a supplemental income that will help you overcome your financial fears during that shift."

"I guess I really need to figure out what I want to do with the rest of my life," replied Meredith.

"Absolutely, and if you truly want to find your purpose and share your gift, you need to begin by determining what factors are causing disturbances in your life. Once you have a clearer vision you must align your life to create the changes you desire. You can only do that by understanding what affects you and the choices that you make. I'm going to send you a questionnaire that will walk you through the eight factors of health so you can break down where your mind goes all the time. Remember that hamster wheel that goes around and around in our minds? Those are often the thoughts that aren't serving us or are holding us back from creating and living our best life. Once you can determine the source of those thoughts, and either debunk or replace them, you will be able to clear space for the thoughts you need in order to find solutions to make something different happen. Meredith, if your thoughts focus on potential failures alone, you will inevitably fail because you're not opening your mind to the steps you need to take to succeed. In other words, you're seeing the problem, not the solution. It's my job to help you see the opportunities and the solutions."

"You're making me believe that there really might be a positive outcome—that maybe I can discover what I'd be really good at and what would make me happy. That's something that's been worrying me. When sales were good, I felt motivated, and I didn't have to consider doing anything different. But now that sales are slow, I am experiencing concern about my future," Meredith said.

"We all worry, but the real question is which worries are real and could potentially occur? When you know which worries are real, you can prepare for them beforehand. I can help you do that," Johanna replied.

The two went on to discuss that process. Johanna explained that there are two major areas of struggle insofar as career changes: financial and emotional.

"Financially, you can make sure you have a safety net to cover your needs until you're solidly on your feet, Meredith. Success is a process of growth, and only you can predict just how much money you will need during your transition. Now, emotionally, I encourage you to focus on the people you surround yourself with. Make sure your family members and the people you are closest to are on the same page and support your decision to embark on this journey of a career change. It will also be important for you to find mentors to support you; if you can find someone who has experience and a solid track record, they can help you understand what to expect. The more you know, the less emotional this process will be."

"Do you have a mentor?" Meredith asked.

"Absolutely. I have three. One is a business mentor, one is a spiritual mentor, and one is my personal mentor. They all bring different points of view and very valid things to the table. You could say that without them Life and Style Coaches would not have the success it has today," Johanna answered.

"How do I find the right people to be my mentors?" Meredith asked.

"Great question! You want your mentors to be experts who are successful in the areas you want to grow, that way they will provide you with the wisdom that comes from their experiences. And where do you find them? They are everywhere; they may even be someone you already know, or people you know could introduce you to them. The people we need in our lives are often closer than we think—after all, there are just a few degrees of separation between us and the rest of the world," Johanna said. "For example, I didn't know you, but through David, we became connected. And now that you're connected to me, you are also connected to the people that I know," Johanna said.

"That's pretty powerful," Meredith pointed out.

"It is extremely powerful; it's the power of proximity. There are people who can help you expedite your success. They are closer and more accessible than you think, Meredith."

As the conversation ended, Meredith pondered Johanna's preliminary suggestions. She would need to create a plan to lay out potential steps she could take in order to successfully make a career shift. She knew that would encounter failures along the way; however, with a positive mindset and preparation, she knew she could succeed. She would need to have a clear understanding of what she wants the new career to entail, get her finances in order and provide herself a safety net to help eliminate her fear of failure. That meant she would need to continue working in her current job, move to a part-time position, or create a stream of supplemental income.

She was excited at the thought of mapping out her life. Johanna was starting to already play a role in shortening the distance from where Meredith was to where she desired to be.

"I think it's time for me to start planning ... for success and for failure!" said Meredith excitedly to herself.

CHAPTER SEVEN

TO BE AMAZING, FIND YOUR WHY

As she said she would, Johanna sent Meredith the questionnaire that would help her determine where her mind goes all the time. She had it open on her computer when her district manager called and asked her to do him a favor—he needed her to attend a veterans' benefit the next weekend in his stead. He knew the man who was organizing the benefit, and it was an important cause, to both him and the company.

Of course, Meredith said yes, but in doing so, she had to make some quick plans for Matthew. Once again, she turned to her parents—her go to whenever she needed support and help.

"Of course, we can watch him," her mom said. "But if it's going to be late, bring his pajamas and have him spend the night. That way, you won't have to wake him up, and he can get a good night's sleep."

Meredith rarely left Matthew overnight, and she always feared that he would be sad or homesick when she was gone. For that reason, she wanted to make it as easy on him as possible, and because she felt guilty when she was away from him, she wanted to make it easier on herself.

The one thing she thought he would miss was their bedtime ritual. Every night, they read a book and she sang him a couple songs. It had been their bedtime routine since he was a baby. She knew she couldn't always be there to read or sing to him personally, but there was something she thought she could do — record those stories and songs and give them to her mom to play at bedtime.

She spent the next three nights recording his favorite story books and childhood songs. When she dropped Matthew off Saturday afternoon, she gave them to her mother.

"I can read to him, Meredith. I can sing, too. You didn't have to do this," her mom said.

"I know. I wanted to. Not only did it make me feel less guilty, I found that I really enjoyed it. It was fun thing to do for my little guy," Meredith said.

After a few hugs and an admonishment not to let her son eat too many treats, Meredith was on the road and on the way to the benefit, where her manager had told her she would meet his friend, Eric Power.

She arrived just as the benefit was starting, and Eric took the stage and thanked everyone for coming. Meredith listened intently as he described his organization and his experience.

Eric explained that he spent 10 years in the service, and got injured in the military and went to the VA disability system, where he found absolutely no help. After spending three or four months going from one place to another, he finally asked a woman about PTSD, his broken back, and many traumatic incidents that happened. He told her that he'd lost faith in the system and was going to figure out how to process his claim on his own. She replied that no veteran was smart enough to figure out how to do that.

Meredith listened as Eric explained that her words made him so angry that he went right to work to prove her wrong and was able to figure out and process his own claim. At the same time, he was going to school and figuring out his future. In a marketing class, he was told to find a service or product that can help a lot of people and create a Facebook page to test it among the people.

The biggest problem he faced was the same one that 19 million veterans faced, which is that they needed help with their VA disability claims. Doing his assignment and creating a small ad, he got 50 leads in one day. His instructor told him to turn it into a business. So he did, and his college assignment became a company called Veterans Disability Help, LLC.

After hearing Eric speak, Meredith couldn't wait to talk to him personally. She found his career path and success fascinating, especially since he was able to help so many people.

"Hi, Eric. I'm Meredith Grant. How are you?"

"Always amazing! Every day above ground is an amazing day, no matter what the world throws at us," he replied.

"I really enjoyed your speech and hearing about your path to entrepreneurism," she said.

"Thank you. It is my passion and my purpose, but as you can imagine, it didn't come without obstacles," he said.

"What type of obstacles did you face, if I can ask?"

Eric explained that finding the right team was one of his biggest obstacles. Having the right people in the right positions was important, but it took time to put that into place. He also indicated that the nature of his business was challenging at times. On a regular basis, he worked with veterans who were struggling with physical, mental, and emotional trauma.

"This is what God put me here on this planet to do. If I didn't get up and go to work, my clients' lives would be affected. I know that we've changed 2,500 veterans' lives for the better. People think it's difficult, but that doesn't matter. I just get up and do it. I've always been the first one to show up, whether it's in boot camp or in the office."

"What is the key to your success, Eric?" Meredith asked.

"I have a mentor who has helped me tremendously. We had both gone through something similar at about the same time. When everyone else was telling me no and that I can't do this, just being around him gave me someone to admire and turn to. I started calling him whenever something went wrong, and as a friend, mentor, and teacher, he helped me persevere. In addition, he introduced me to his friends and mentors, and I became friends with them and learned a lot from them."

"The more I was around them, the more I wanted to know them and learn from them. Birds of a feather flock together.

People are social creatures, and we learn from each other. That is true in what I do. In addition to everything they've taught me, I've become a part of a team once again, which helped build my confidence. Because I've been in the space of this mentor and his associates, I've made emotional connections, as well."

"Meredith, it's not easy starting out, and when you're on your own and starting a business, you need to remember your 'why.' Now that I've become a mentor to others, I encourage them to find their why. Especially if you hit a rough patch or a wall, you need your why to help you figure out how to get around, over, under or through that wall. I've found my spot, and I tell people they need to be in the right spot, where they know they are going to learn from the people and successes around them."

"That's good advice, Eric. You're an inspiration, and I'd like to learn from you and your success. It also sounds like you have some incredible friends and mentors," Meredith pointed out.

"If I can help you, I'll be happy to. I've made my life's work all about helping people. It's been amazing. When I remember that, I remind myself that I am also always amazing. And I'm always strong. I'm not afraid of work, and I strive to work through the issues and problems. I've discovered that everything is usually going to be fine. That is especially true for veterans," he said.

"I'm exploring the idea of becoming an entrepreneur someday, Eric. You've taught me a lot in such a short time. Thank you," Meredith said.

"If I can offer one more piece of advice, Meredith, it's don't be afraid to fail, and stand your ground when you know you are correct. Don't let that fear keep you from finding your purpose," he said.

"I'm beginning to learn that. Thank you, Eric, and thank you for what you do to help other veterans. I wish I could find something that would make such a worthwhile impact," she said.

"You can. Find a common problem or need and create a solution for all the people affected by it. You might already know what it is. But if you don't, you will. When you do, it will be amazing."

CHAPTER EIGHT

FINDING YOUR IDENTITY

Meredith didn't want to take advantage of her mother, so she woke up bright and early Sunday morning to pick up Matthew and relieve her mom. Quickly showering, she decided to forego her morning routine and let her hair dry naturally, knowing it would invite the uncontrollable curls she fought to tame every morning before she went to work. After all, she didn't have any formal plans for the day, just spending time with Matthew and getting her weekend chores out of the way.

Her mom didn't fail to notice that she hadn't made a great effort with her appearance, but to her surprise, her mother voiced her approval. Meredith, you should wear your hair like that more often. Your curls are so pretty. I don't know why you spend so much time straightening them. You should leave it natural all the time," her mom said.

"Mom, I straighten my hair because curls tend to look messy. Straight hair is easier to tame, and it looks more professional," Meredith sighed.

"Well, I like this look better—even your clothes. You look much more relaxed and approachable than you do when you go to work," her mother remarked.

The statement took Meredith aback for a brief moment. She'd never considered herself to be uptight or unapproachable, and her mom's comment made her wonder if others perceived her that way, too. Sighing, she wrote it off as her mother's well-intentioned criticism and changed the subject.

"So, Mom, how was Matthew for you?"

"He was great. He's such a good boy, Meredith. But he does tend to miss you when he gets sleepy. It helped to play the songs and stories you recorded. We listened to a few of those, and he fell fast asleep. I didn't hear a peep from him until this morning," her mom replied.

"Good, I was hoping those would come in handy," Meredith said.

"It was just like you were here. He even sang along with you a time or two. Actually, I forgot what a pretty voice you have. I haven't heard you sing since high school," her mom remarked.

"Well, I still sing for this little man," she said, rubbing her hand across her son's dark hair. "At least, while he'll still let me."

Returning home, she started a load of laundry and played a couple games with Matthew before putting him down for a short nap. When everything was quiet, her mind wandered back to her mother's comments, and she wondered if there was any truth to it. Picking up her phone, she called her sister, Emily, and asked if she felt the same.

"I've always loved your curls, Mer, so I might not be the best person to ask. I think Mom meant well and wasn't trying to be critical. Maybe you just took it personally," Emily suggested.

"She came just short of saying that I am stuffy; she even said I don't look approachable," Meredith countered.

"That sounds like Mom," her sister laughed. "Maybe she just wishes you would be a little more carefree, like you were when you were a kid. We were exact opposites, weren't we? I was the athletic one, always playing sports and into fitness, while you were the one who walked around without a care in the world, singing and dancing all the time?"

"Yes, but I'm an adult now. I'm a mother, and I have responsibilities," Meredith replied.

"I know that. But maybe Mom's right and you've forgotten who you are. I'm a mother, too, but I still make it a point to run every day and go to my yoga classes. When is the last time you did anything for fun, Meredith?"

"It's been a while, but ..."

"No excuses! You need to reset your vibration and get out of the house. Hey, I have an idea. Why don't you come to yoga with me on Wednesday? Daniel is going to be there, and I think he can help you," Emily said.

"What are you talking about, reset my vibration? And who's Daniel?"

"Don't worry about it. We haven't had a girls' night in ages, and I won't take no for an answer. Matthew can come over here and play with his cousins. They had a blast at Mom's last night," Emily remarked.

"Yes, he must have been worn out. Mom said he got a little overtired and started to miss me," Meredith replied.

"Don't feel guilty. She played some of your songs, and he was just fine. Hey, I need a copy of that—maybe it will put my kids to sleep like it did Matthew!" she laughed.

"I can send it to you as soon as we hang up," Meredith laughed.

"Perfect. And don't forget Wednesday—be here at 5:30. Yoga starts at 6:00, and I don't want to be late."

CHAPTER NINE

PUSH YOUR EDGE, NOT YOUR BUTTONS

"Wow, Meredith, I love your hair!" her assistant, Charlotte exclaimed when she walked in the office Monday morning. "I wish I could curl my hair like that!"

"They're natural, Charlotte. I decided not to fight them this morning."

"Well, I like the change. You should wear your hair like that more often."

"Thank you, Charlotte. Apparently, my mom and sister agree with you," Meredith sighed.

"Hey, how was the benefit Saturday night?"

"I really enjoyed it. It's such a worthwhile organization, Charlotte. After meeting Eric Power and hearing about what they do, I'm inspired to help our veterans, too. That reminds me, I need to send him a thank you for his hospitality," Meredith replied.

She sat down and composed a quick email to Eric, complimenting him on the success of his benefit and thanking him for taking the time to talk to her and sharing his story. She concluded her email with, "I am inspired to lend my time and efforts to those who have served. I'll be in touch soon."

It was a good start to the week. For a Monday, it was an upbeat morning, followed by a fruitful afternoon of meetings that produced two new clients. Hoping it was the beginning of an upward trend, Meredith used the momentum to reconnect with existing clients about updating their insurance policies.

By the time she got off work Wednesday, though, she was beginning to wane. After starting the week on good note, she hadn't been able to sustain her success. In the last two days, she hadn't gained any additional clients, and to add to her disappointment, one client even canceled his appointment.

It had been a long afternoon, and Meredith wished she could go home and do nothing, but she knew her sister would never forgive her if she canceled their plans. Besides, Matthew was excited about spending the evening with his cousins. It was all he had talked about for the last three days.

Resigning herself to make the best of it, she dropped Matthew off with his uncle and cousins, promising not to be gone too long.

To Meredith's surprise, she enjoyed the yoga class. Just as Krystylle Richardson had told her, being quiet and still cleared her mind. Although she wasn't seasoned at practicing yoga, she had to admit that she could see the benefits after just one session.

When the class was over, Emily grabbed her arm and pulled her out of the room.

"Mer, look, there's Daniel. Let's go talk to him and grab a smoothie," she said, as she led the way to a man sitting at the juice counter.

"Hi, Daniel!" Emily exclaimed, excited to see her friend. "I want you to meet my sister, Meredith. Mer, this is my friend, Daniel Mangena."

Emily didn't miss a beat while they exchanged hellos. "Daniel, I told Meredith that she really needs to reset her vibration, and I just know you're the person who can help her do it."

"I'm sorry," Meredith immediately apologized. "I didn't intend to have Emily bombard you and ask you to step in and work on my vibration, whatever that is."

"It might not be what you intended, but if you're interested in talking about intentions, I'm your guy,"

"Oh? What do you do, Daniel?" Meredith asked.

"I work predominantly around intention setting and helping people create alignment with their goals. The basis of my work is that when we set clear intentions, which are really how we want to feel at the end of the day, it enables us to step into a space where we can feel a connection to that experience. Once we can do that, we are better able to visualize and mentally rehearse it. Then we can begin to make choices that brings us closer to that goal or intention and the mindset and practicality that is demanded of us in order to create real results in our life."

"Do you mean that we can really decide how we want to feel at the end of the day and make that happen?" Meredith asked.

"Yes, Meredith. In order to do that, though, we need to have clear direction for the power we have within us to create results. You see, our minds are always working and always setting goals for us, either consciously or unconsciously. But when we set intentions, we destruct the autopilot that has been creating the results we've been experiencing, and it puts us in a space where we can actually direct that intention."

"That's interesting. How does it work?" Meredith asked, sitting forward in her chair.

"Our mind is always giving reality a blueprint of what we are going to experience. When we set intentions, we actually dictate what that blueprint will be, rather than letting it run on autopilot based on our preprogrammed experiences based on our subconscious," explained Daniel.

"Like I said, it is based on our emotions. The first point of call for us to experience where we are in terms of our frequency and energy is our feelings. When we are deliberate in how we feel, we can direct where our frequency is," he added.

"What does this have to do with resetting my vibration?" Meredith asked.

"Well, one of the universal laws is the Law of Vibration, which some people mistake for the Law of Attraction, which is based on getting what you are and think. Really, the Law of Vibration is what matters because what we really we end up experiencing is what our vibration matches up to," he said.

"That sounds fascinating, but I'm not familiar with my vibration or how I can change it," Meredith admitted.

"Let me explain. There is research that shows we are essentially electromagnets; one comes out of our mind, and one comes out of our heart. Everything has an electromagnet signal. Now, many people know what they want, so they pray, meditate, practice yoga, or go to an energy healer, and then wonder why they're not getting the results they want. Those things are all good, but they're not enough. To get the results they want, they have to do more. They have to follow through and believe that it is possible, which is where the mindset comes in."

"That makes sense, Daniel," Meredith mused.

"And here's why: We can only mentally rehearse it or experience it if we believe it is possible. Otherwise, a part of the brain shuts off because it doesn't believe what we want is possible. This happens with opportunities in our businesses and our lives. It also happens with the good qualities of people we are around or the bad qualities of people we are convincing ourselves to stay around. For instance, it's that way when someone is in a bad relationship and people say the person is no good, but the other person cannot see those bad qualities because their brain is shut off from seeing it. The same is true in regard to what we want to create—we cannot see the road to it because we don't believe we can create it."

"What's the best way to create that belief?" Meredith asked.

"It's important to surround yourself with people, places, and things that support the outcome you want to experience. For example, if you surround yourself with an environment of poverty, you create inputs of poverty in the mind, and when you try to mentally rehearse abundance, you will come up amok. You need to surround yourself with the things that reinforce what you actually want," Daniel explained.

"It all starts with our intentions. Once we set clear intentions, we can identify the inputs associated with that intention. Ask yourself what type of people you should talk to, what books you should read, what movies you should watch, and what places should you go to give yourself input to support this new outcome," he said.

"So, I need to put the things into my life that support what I want, right?"

"At its core, what we're doing is shifting away from the mind's default program by giving it evidence to the contrary, evidence that supports the outcome we desire. Once we do that effectively, the mental rehearsal can begin, and it starts to set the mind up to look for opportunities and being able to activate them."

"I think I get it! We have to make a conscious effort to change our unconscious thoughts. Is that correct?"

"It's part of it. The mind will always revert back to default, so we have to do the work of resetting that default if we don't want to go back to the results we've always gotten. However, like I said, these results are only possible if we take action. From my experience, this is where people struggle. They'll read a load of books and go to courses and get coaching, but they won't take action—or they'll do the frequency work and get emotional about what they want, but unless they follow through with actions and choices that are consistent with the intention, vibration, and mental rehearsal, they won't be able to take the action necessary to get the result."

"The great thing is, when everything is lined up, the action part is a piece of cake. I like to say that the inner game has to be taken care of before the outer game. When the inner work is done, it will facilitate the actual experience happening more spontaneously, which is effectively how we create the results," Daniel said. "I've been working with Emily, and she's made great progress in resetting her vibration."

"He's right, Mer. Once I really focused on it, it made a big difference for me," Emily added. Push your edge, but don't push your buttons. Find the limit of where you are.

"Like I told Emily, though, you need to know your limits. When you are creating new belief systems and new feelings and taking action, find your edge and push it. It will be a bit uncomfortable, but be careful not to push your buttons. If you do, you will end up going back to the beginning. I've seen it many times. People go to take action, and they get scared and take no action at all, or they haven't created the foundation or done the groundwork to support it, so they slide all the way back. That's why I encourage people to take baby steps to where they want to go. I call this process 'micro-shiftin', which is just taking a consistent series of baby steps in the direction of our intended outcome. It will bring growth in a manner you can sustain over time," Daniel explained.

"It's like yoga or exercise, Meredith. You get better at it the more you do it. For example, if you exercise for 10 minutes a day, every day, for a month, your capacity for exercise will increase. You can build that consistency in training your mind, too, and expand your capacity over time. Your edge will naturally expand when you move against it in micro shifts," he added.

"Daniel, I think just talking with you has raised my vibration! It's enlightening to really believe that I have control over the results I receive," Meredith exclaimed.

"Yes, you can make your goals and dreams a reality. However, I always tell people to dream with their eyes open. You should have big dreams and big goals, but don't be blind to the fact that you have to take action and do something about it," he said.

"Now I just have to figure out precisely what I need to do," Meredith commented.

"I already told you—it's as simple as setting your intention and creating your alignment so you believe it and can mentally rehearse it. The universe will do the rest, matching your results to your vibration."

CHAPTER TEN

YOU HAVE A PARACHUTE

The next week, Meredith was surprised, but happy, to receive a text message from Shannon Parsons.

"Hi, Meredith! I hope you're doing well. Reaching out to see if you might be interested in talking to another friend of mine — single mom to single mom. She's great, and I think she can provide some helpful advice about your struggles in that part of your life. She really has a lot to offer. Let me know!"

Meredith quickly replied, "It's great to hear from you, Shannon. A friend of yours is a friend of mine. I'd love to talk to her!"

"Great. Her name is Tatjana Omanovic. She's a real hero! I'll have her get a hold of you."

Tatjana reached out to Meredith the next day, and the two scheduled a phone call for later that week. Meredith quickly found that Shannon was right—Tatjana did have an expansive past and a rich history. However, it was her genuine compassion that touched Meredith the most.

"As a single parent, Meredith, I really wanted to reach out to you. Right now, I'm a full-time mother, but I was an active duty Marine. I retired several years ago to help my sons transition through their teen years. It's difficult to be a present mother when you're deployed to a war zone," Tatjana explained.

"I can imagine. I don't know how you managed to be a parent while serving," Meredith replied.

"It was difficult, and I struggled with being away from my boys. But I really wanted to talk to you because I've been through so much in my life that during the last several years, I've been feeling an urgency to help others. There is so much happening in the world, and it's changing quickly. People are losing themselves and veering off course. Because I've been through so much, I hope I can help others," Tatjana said.

"I'd like to hear about that," Meredith encouraged.

"Well, here's the short version. I've slept in cars and under bridges. I've had no food and been without citizenship or even a green card. I got married, and then my husband had cancer. Thankfully, he survived, and we had twins. But then, we divorced, and I became a single mom," Tatjana said.

"Wow, how'd you do it?" Meredith asked.

"Having grown up in old Yugoslavia and in Serbia, I'm no stranger to living without. It helped me realize that money doesn't make us rich. Life is about the relationships we discover along the way, and the most important relationship is the one with myself. I learned from my father that the greatest resource we have is people."

"When my dad was diagnosed with cancer, he left to get treatment, and I stayed behind to take care of my grandmother. It was a lot of responsibility, and I didn't have any real diversions. In school, I didn't have a lot of friends. But then I joined a kayaking team and found an outlet that gave me a lot of energy and insight," she said.

"I worked really hard, Meredith, and became a national champion and made it to the Hopeful Olympics for Barcelona in 1992. But the civil war broke out in 1989, and I had been applying for a visa at the consulate. After being denied seven times, I tried again, changing my application strategy and was approved on the spot.

"That's amazing. It must have been difficult for you," Meredith replied.

"It was. At the time, my father was in Florida and was taking any job he could find. Actually, he created opportunities, and they turned into jobs. I learned a lot from him. That's how I found the opportunity to serve in the Marines," Tatjana explained.

"How did that happen?"

"I had been in Pompano Beach for four years, and one day, I was working out at the beach when I was approached by two Marines. They asked me what I did and whether I was interested in joining the Marines," Tatjana said, then laughed.

"Meredith, they had to tell me what 'the Marines' was; I didn't have any idea. But when they explained it, I thought it was great—they were going to pay me to work out! But I told them I had to wait a month or two until I got my green card, which arrived about a month later, and I joined. At the time, I didn't think I was joining for 20 years; I just wanted to join for four years at a time, as a way of saying thank you and giving back to this country that was giving me opportunities and a second chance at life. It was a way to find out what this country is about and feel the true heartbeat of the country," Tatjana told her.

"I told you before that the most important relationship I've had is the one I have with myself. I learned a lot in the Marines. One thing was to keep myself at a higher standard and always be at ready. Most Marines met at 5:15 a.m. to run as a unit, a company. While others were out partying and socializing, I was in bed at 7:30 p.m., so I could get up at 12:30 and do my own five-mile run, always trying to improve my speed. I always tried to be faster and better. I did what I could to get noticed, being on time, even early for everything, and I was always prepared. It was an honor to me to have that job and that opportunity. So in my case, I succeeded by the basics: getting plenty of sleep, being prepared, and avoiding making choices that would have affected my ability to do that."

"The Marines served me well, especially after my husband and I divorced," Tatjana said. "My husband became abusive, and I had to make the best choices for me and my children. As a single mother, everything was tough. I understood I had to be the mom and the dad, the grandma and grandpa, and the uncle and the aunt. I was grateful that I had my kids and *got* to be all of those roles, even when times were rough. For example, Meredith, when I explained to my kids that we didn't have enough money for something, they'd step in and help. My son was eight years old when he learned to balance a checkbook! My boys looked out for me and would forego new things to make it easier for me," Tatjana said.

"I'm scared that my son will have to go without, too," Meredith admitted.

"Don't be scared. Be honest. Kids really are capable of being a part of the family unit, and it makes the family stronger. Parenting can be difficult, but sometimes we need to stay quiet so we can regroup and recalibrate and reinvent ourselves—for ourselves and what fits us and our family. It's part of being authentic. Someone out there will find value in that, even if it is just one person. That's why I hoped my story could help you in some way, Meredith."

"You are incredibly kind, Tatjana."

"I will do anything I can to help others, especially if I know they're in need. There were times, though, when I had to put on a stone face and freeze my heart while I was deployed for nine months at a time. But even then, it warmed my heart to help people in other countries who were suffering, not by their choice," Tatjana explained.

"I cannot imagine how difficult, but rewarding, that was," Meredith replied.

"It was. I was gone frequently when I was in the Marines, but when I came home and became a life coach, I realized I was gone even more. I kept trying to drum up business and a following, but I didn't have a tribe at the time. I couldn't sustain on my own, and I knew it. I also knew my kids took precedence over anything else. The most important business in my life at that time was my children. I needed to work on them. I just knew that I'd spent too much time away from them, and I couldn't get it back," Tatjana admitted.

"Right now, what you're doing benefits your son, too. Like me, I'm sure you know he's being taken care of when you're gone. After 20 years, though, I knew I'd given my best, but I didn't want to lose value as a mom. Business could wait, and this was my opportunity to focus on me and my children," Tatjana explained.

"If you want to succeed, Meredith, you need to define success. Do it on your terms. As long as you're doing your best and know that you've given your best, that's all that matters. The business will always be there, but these years with your son won't be," said Tatjana. "Focus on yourself and your grounding. Have gratitude for every person you meet every day. Be vulnerable and open with them, and they will value you more. Don't lose yourself, because if you do, you can't make rational decisions. Allow yourself to be human and reach within so you can make decisions with a clear conscience. You have to connect to yourself, and you have to disconnect from what everyone else wants and expects in order to do that and be real.

"Relationships are everything, Meredith. People need to know you, but in a world where we connect virtually, we've lost the capability of being real and making real connections. But in connecting, we create the relationships and genuineness that produce success. By helping others, we renew and anew ourselves, which gives us strength," Tatjana said with compassion.

"You are so wise, Tatjana. Looking at your life, my troubles seem small," Meredith said.

"It's not always about ourselves. When we look at other people's problems, we can see that our problem isn't so large, after all. And when we zoom out and look at ourselves from another planet, removed from the situation, we can see our problems in their true perspective and see that there are solutions we didn't see before," Tatjana said.

"Tatjana, I can relate to so much of what you said. I don't think I can express just how much you've helped me and touched my heart ... and I don't really know you," Meredith said.

"I just hope my experiences can in some way help people," Tatjana said with so much earnest that her voice broke.

"Just talking to you has helped me. It's like you're an angel that was sent my way," Meredith replied.

"Thank you. Actually, that reminds me of a story. Do you have a minute to talk a little more, Meredith?"

"Yes, I'd love to hear it."

"In 2013, I was in Starbucks on Veteran's Day, and a gentleman was in the line after me. He was about 70 years old, and he was a Vietnam veteran. I later learned his name was Angel. I told the cashier that I was leaving five dollars to apply to his order. I left and was getting in my car when he ran out after me, thanking me for the cup of coffee that was in his hand. He told me I didn't have to do that, and I thanked him for serving. He thanked me for valuing and seeing him. In our conversation, he learned that I was a Marine and a single mom, and we connected. He gave me his card, but I never called him. I was just too busy."

"Two weeks later, it was the day before Thanksgiving, and a friend called me. He said he had duty the next day, but his two-year-old child was having heart surgery. Could I take his place? Without hesitating, I said of course. Then, I realized I had no one to take my kids overnight. Then I remembered that I had met a single father two weeks before when we both of our kids were skating at the park. As a last resort, I called and explained the situation to him. He didn't think twice and told me to bring my kids to his house."

"When I got off duty, he had been taking care of my kids for 36 hours. It was Thanksgiving morning, and I wanted to pick up my kids. But when I walked out, I saw a Jeep parked near the doors at the battalion and a child sleeping in it. I walked back in and asked the guy who relieved me if it was his truck and his kid. He said yes, the child was going to be there with him that day.

"Learning that the child was six years old, I asked to meet him, saying he could come with me and my boys for the day. Although I'm a complete stranger, his son came with me to pick up my kids. When we arrived, my new friend suggested we take all of our kids to a skate park, where a little white dog walked up to me. She was cold, shivering, and full of fleas. When it was time to go, my son ran to the car and grabbed a blanket, saying we were taking her home."

"Meredith, I'd finished a 36-hour duty. I had my kids and someone else's child with me, and now I had this little dog. Keep in mind that there wasn't a stuffed turkey and potatoes waiting in the oven at home for Thanksgiving dinner. So when the kids suggested we stop to buy dog food at the grocery store, I agreed. In the same aisle, I run into Angel, the veteran I met at Starbucks," Tatjana said.

"You're kidding!"

"No. He asked what I was doing with all those kids, and I explained how I'd been working and had just found this dog. We were getting her some food and were going home to make some sandwiches. He said, 'No, you're not. You're all coming to my house for Thanksgiving dinner, and I'm calling some other Marines and their families, too.' He called his wife and told her we were coming.

"Meredith, his house was on Daisy Lane, just three minutes away from my house. We went and had a great time. We all laughed and cried together in Angel's house, with his family and the families of servicemembers and veterans he invited."

"That's a beautiful story," Meredith whispered.

"We are still connected with Angel. He's important to me and my children. We even named our dog 'Daisy' after the street Angel lives on. It's a way of paying tribute to him and the wonderful people we met on that Thanksgiving Day. And none of this would have ever happened, Meredith, if our days and lives hadn't been impacted by our desire to help one person we connected with," Tatjana explained. "What started out to be an imperfect, uneventful Thanksgiving became an opportunity for all of us to help and make a lasting impression on each other."

"You've made a lasting impression on me, Tatjana," Meredith said.

"We're nothing without other humans. If there are no difficulties, what is life? We have to trust others. Sure, there will be times things don't go the way we want, but what if they connect you with the connector of connectors? What if you start the business of your dreams and your dream team shows up because you spoke about your dreams to the right people at the right time? They might be the parachute you need when you're vulnerable and need help. They will open your parachute for you … and when you help others, you become stronger and can open your own parachute," Tatjana said. "By connecting and serving, I know I can open my own parachute. You can, too, Meredith. Trust in that."

CHAPTER ELEVEN

YOU ARE IN CONTROL OF YOUR CHALLENGES

Tatjana gave Meredith a new perspective, and in turn, Meredith gave herself permission not to feel guilty about not being enough or doing enough. There were times, though, when she struggled with it. Old habits were hard to break.

In the meantime, she focused on finding her purpose. The more she learned, the more it became apparent to her that insurance was her vocation, but not her passion.

They kept in touch, emailing and texting from time to time. It was apparent to Meredith that Tatjana didn't just meet people; she connected with them on a deep and genuine level.

The two continued to keep in touch. During one of their phone calls, Meredith expressed her discouragement with the progress she was making in her career. Things were improving, but not at the pace she would like. In talking to her fellow insurance agents, she learned they were also facing the same struggles.

"I guess this is new territory for me, Tatjana. For several years, everything went smoothly. I never had to deal with adversity. I'm not sure I know how to turn things around," Meredith confessed.

"Krysten!" Tatjana exclaimed.

"What? Who is Krysten?" Meredith asked.

"She's a friend, and if anyone can tell you about adversity, Krysten Maracle can! I just know she can help you! I'll text you her number. Give her a call!"

It took a couple days for Meredith to get the nerve to contact Krysten, but Krysten immediately put her at ease. She was so easy to talk to, and Meredith sensed immediately that she was one of the most genuine people she'd ever talked to.

When Meredith asked Krysten about herself, Krysten gave her a brief history. Born and raised in sunny San Diego, she was brought up in a good family and had a good education. It had always been ingrained in her that she would go to college, but by her own admission, she wasn't studious.

"But then my parents divorced when I was 13, and I moved to a foreign land—all the way across the country to Pennsylvania. It was a culture shock! Let's just say it built my character," Krysten laughed.

"It changed my life," Krysten added. "It was a pivotal moment. In Pennsylvania, I attended what was akin to a private school, and they made me take an entrance exam to get into high school. And I failed because they said I was 'not smart enough.' Actually, they found out I had dyslexia, so they held me back a grade."

"Meredith, here I was, a little girl completely out of her zone and now I had a label on me. I thought it was ridiculous and vowed to do well in school. After never having studied in my life, I turned things around and got good grades and was in the Honor Society," Krysten explained.

"Good for you! How did you turn things around so quickly?" Meredith asked.

"I guess I'm a fighter. Actually, I fight back. If someone says I can't do something, I come back with 'Oh, just watch me!'" she laughed. "And it's a good thing. Otherwise, I might be homeless and jobless. It wasn't easy, but I became smart, but lazy smart. For example, I wouldn't read *The Canterbury Tales*, but I would read and study the cliff notes."

"I became a computer science major in college. As a girl, it was a nontraditional career. Before my senior year, I decided I wanted to return to California, so I transferred to San Diego State, where I graduated with honors. After that, I got a job with the Navy as a civilian in computer science, where I stayed for 30 years before retiring just this year," Krysten advised.

"That's quite a career. What are you doing now that you're retired, Krysten?"

"I have plans to do a lot of travelling. It's something I've always loved to do. I spent years as a single mom, raising my two kids, and now that they're grown and out of college, I can expand my travels. But I've also started my own company, Maracle Masterminds. I've also been very involved with Greg Reid's events," Krysten said. "I heard you went to his last event, Meredith."

"I did! And I loved it. The people were great, and through them, I've been meeting even more fantastic people," Meredith responded.

"That's what we're here for. We all want to help people. I'm fortunate that today I can help people and give back. So, Meredith, how can I help you?"

"For the first time, Krysten, I'm seeing a lull in my career. I don't know if I can turn it around, or if I should try. Maybe it's a lost cause. At the same time, I'm not comfortable taking risks because I have a four-year-old son. I've never dealt with adversity, but I've been told you have and might have some insight that could help me," Meredith answered.

"Everyone's situation is different. I know the difficulties of being a mother and how trying it can be. There will be challenges, and some you won't be prepared for. You have to parent in the best way you know. My advice, and it applies to parenting and life, is to take control and never give up. Giving up isn't an option for me. I had three miscarriages before I had my first child, and people were telling me to consider adoption. I wouldn't give up, and I did have the two children I wanted. That's one thing you'll learn about me is that I refuse to give up!" Krysten said.

"It must have been a trying time," Meredith remarked.

"I'll admit it was very traumatic, but I just knew it was going to work out. Then when I got divorced, I knew that would be difficult, too, but I also knew I could start over. I approach everything in life with that attitude. People are afraid to take chances because they're afraid it won't work out the way they want. But whatever you decide to do, if you want it bad enough, it will work out," Krysten assured her. "Doing what's right for you won't always be easy, but it will be worth it."

"How do you entice yourself to push through when it gets challenging?" Meredith asked.

"I bribe myself," Krysten laughed. "No, really, I do actually tell myself that if I finish something, I can get a reward. It works for me. To this day, I still buy myself flowers on a regular basis."

"You're so optimistic, Krysten. I wish I could be more like you," Meredith said.

"Optimism is a choice. I've had a lot of adversity and challenges in my life, and if I can choose to be optimistic, I know you can, too. We only get one life, Meredith, and we shouldn't deprive ourselves of every opportunity to enjoy it. It's all a choice—remember this: you are in control—nobody else is. It took me a while to learn that. When I was young, I catered to everyone else and, boy, did I get run over. I had to learn to take care of myself and my family and not worry about anyone else or what they thought. Some people might tell you to play it safe and that, as a mother, it's not a good time to start over. Let me tell you, it's never too late to start over. It's never too late to reinvent your life. You might be a mother, but that doesn't mean you can't also be successful and happy."

"Thank you. I never thought of it that way, Krysten," Meredith responded.

"You'll be fine, Meredith. You have to believe that. Challenges come for a reason, and this is your opportunity to find out what those reasons are and take control. I did, and I know you can, too. Remember, too, that it helps to have people with experience to turn to for support and advice. For that purpose, I'd like you to attend a Maracle Mastermind event. If you like it, you can join our amazing group and become a Maracle Mastermind member."

"That would be awesome, Krysten! I'll be sure to take you up on that invitation! Thank you!" Meredith exclaimed.

CHAPTER TWELVE

INVENTING YOUR FUTURE

That night, she and Matthew went through their usual bedtime ritual and she read him their special bedtime stories, sometimes several times, before he finally went to sleep. Then she finished some household chores and preparations for the next day before giving in to some much needed sleep. However, she was surprised that sleep didn't come easily. Her mind was too busy working overtime, taking in everything she'd learned and the advice she'd been given.

Her mom and sister believed she'd lost her former self and had forgotten the things that once brought her joy. She'd been fortunate to meet some terrific people who shared their advice, and she knew it would be put to good use ... if only she knew what to do.

Daniel Mangena had said that our minds are always working and setting intentions for us. But she needed to clear her mind; maybe then, the answers would come.

Through meditation, a state of relaxation came over her, and instead of controlling her mind, she decided to let it go where it wanted. However, her mind kept returning to home, and she visualized herself cuddling up next to her son and reading his bedtime stories. That didn't surprise her; after all, it was when she was most content and felt that for that moment, all was right with the world.

The next morning, she was in the shower when it hit her. It was an aha moment where everything seemed to come together, and suddenly, it all made sense! Meredith had an idea, and it was like she'd been led to it all along.

After dropping Matthew off at preschool, she called Michele Malo, hoping she might have some answers.

"Hi, Michele. It's Meredith Grant. I know it's early, but I have an idea and need some help," she said.

"Sure, what do you need?" Michele asked.

"I have an idea for a new business, but I don't know anything about starting a new business or creating products and bringing them to market. This is really new territory for me, but I remembered that you started a whole new career and know what it takes. I was hoping you might know the right person who could give me some advice," Meredith stated.

"You sound excited, Meredith. Do you want to share your idea with me?" Michele asked.

"Not just yet. But I wondered if you know anyone who has ever done anything like this before who could give me some advice on how to get started."

"Hmm, I'm not sure, Meredith. Oh, wait! I do know someone. He's actually invented a few things! His name is David Blackford, and he's a really nice guy. Let me reach out to him, and I'll get back to you as soon as I can," Michele offered.

Although Meredith was anxious, she began her day. There were a few voicemails with clients who had questions about submitting a claim and a couple emails that she needed to respond to. One expressed interest in talking to her about home, auto, and life insurance, so she replied immediately with an invitation to set up an appointment. Over all, it was an encouraging start to the day.

It was late afternoon when she heard from Michele.

"Hey, Meredith, I called David, and he's out of town right now. But he will be available after Wednesday. Grab a pen, and I'll give you his number. He said he'll be looking for your call," she said.

After putting a note in her calendar to call David on Thursday, Meredith reached out to a friend, Eric Figueroa. If David could steer her in the right direction, she was going to need to talk to Eric.

She waited until Thursday evening to call David Blackford and gave him an overview of her idea.

"Michele told me you're an inventor and have brought products to market. I was hoping you could give me some advice. I don't know where to start," Meredith said.

"Yes, I am an inventor and have learned a lot about bringing a product to market. Coincidentally, one of my goals is to be able to teach others how to do it, even children. I'm already in the process of helping my daughter start her own business," David remarked.

"That's wonderful! David, I don't know where to start or even what questions to ask. So maybe you can take the lead here," Meredith suggested.

"Okay. I can see that you need to know the first steps in turning an idea into a prototype of your product, but if you're open to it, I can also offer you some entrepreneurial advice," he said..

"Of course! So where do we start?"

"Meredith, I am an inventor, but I still have my day job. As a product development specialist, I know it can take time to create and perfect a product, find funding, and bring it to market. For example, it took three years, but we just finished our first shipment on my most recent invention," David said.

David shared some specifics she would need to know to begin. His first recommendation was to get a firm vision of the product she wanted. From there, she needed to create a prototype.

They talked for an hour, and Meredith had pages of notes when they were done. Then, David told her that the greatest product could fail if she didn't have the entrepreneurial skills to succeed. However, he wasn't discouraging her in any way — he was excited and wanted to prepare her for what she would need to know.

"You need to have a firm vision and grasp of what your business will be. The philosophies behind it are very important and critical to your success. I've been an entrepreneur my whole life, and I knew what a profit was when I was just six years old. I used to go door to door, selling greeting cards and wrapping paper. I washed windows when I was a child. And I know what it takes to generate money," he said.

"What advice would you give me?" Meredith asked.

"My biggest piece of advice is that you need to be grateful for what you already have. You have everything inside you to move forward and the resources and people to make it happen. You've got to put in the work, but when you put some effort into it, you can be a success, Meredith. That might mean you have to get out of your comfort zone and find people you wouldn't normally meet. For example, I am part of the San Diego Inventors Forum, but if it wasn't for my mentor, I wouldn't have known the association exists. I've met so many people that I wouldn't have known unless I'd gone out and looked for things. It takes due diligence, but you'll find what you need if you expand your circle," David advised.

"I can see that, David, because my idea wouldn't have come to me at all if it wasn't for the fact that I did increase my circle!" Meredith exclaimed.

"Often, it's the people around you who inspire you and bring you answers. Sometimes, it's your challenges. For example, my idea came to me while selling real estate. I had an open house scheduled and put some of those directional signs on the street to direct people to the house, but the wind always blows them down. I came up with a product that anchors those signs, and they can be used in other industries, too, like construction, road signs, and even advertisements. Identify a problem and find a solution, and you have a product and an invention," he said.

"That's great! I hope your invention is a success!" Meredith said.

"Oh, it will be. I'm doing it. It's not a hope. One thing you'll learn about me is that I'm not a quitter. My wife calls me unstoppable," he shared. "Sure, there is a chance it might not be as successful as I want, but if that happens, it will be just another learning lesson. But I will figure out a way to make it work. I know I can still get there, but I just have to get there a different way," David said.

"That's a wonderful attitude, David."

"Let me tell you a story. I met a guy once who talked about the path to our destination. Success doesn't always take a straight line—sometimes you have to detour and take a few different turns to get to your destination. Instead of a straight line, you might have a wavy line that zig zags all over. It doesn't matter how much zig zagging you have to do, as long as you reach your destination."

"So, when you have to try something different, or if something doesn't work, how do you counter that?" Meredith asked.

"You have to get quiet and think about your other options. Getting creative in the process is so important. Your subconscious is so huge. You can go to bed and not have the answers, but wake up with a new idea. Don't tell me you've never been in the shower at some time, not even thinking about your problems, and suddenly, there's your answer! You can't wait to get out of the shower to try it out," David exclaimed.

"You are so right, David. That's exactly how I came up with my idea—I got quiet the night before and tried to set my intention, and the next morning, it came to me in the shower!"

"Amazing, isn't it? Another tactic I learned from a mentor is to take a walk and look far away, then look at something close. Repeat that as you go along on your walk, and you'll see how it clears your mind. It sounds simple, but it really works!"

"Interesting. I'll have to try that," Meredith replied.

"It's my gift to you."

"Thank you. David, we've been on the phone for a while now, and I don't want to keep you too long. Before we hang up, is there anything else I need to know?" she asked.

"You have to know enough to know that you don't know everything. I've learned that you need to have a high teachability index, especially when it comes to inventing something new and doing things you've never done before," he said.

"I think I have a lot to learn," Meredith quipped.

"You will learn a lot, but there are reasons the lessons come your way. Everything happens for you; it doesn't happen to you. There are reasons things happen. You won't know what they are, but someday in hindsight, you will realize that it happened so you could learn from it." David said. "Don't let those things hold you back. We are put here to do two things: to serve and to be happy. Don't forget the happiness part of it.

I assure you, if you remember to serve and be happy, you will have a prosperous life."

"David, I think you're right. I've met some people who have truly served—they've served our country. And they are now focused on helping others. It hasn't been easy for them, but they are happy and fulfilled."

"When you serve and are happy, you're anchored. And when you're anchored and believe in yourself, anything can happen," David added.

"You've given me so much to think about, and I can't thank you enough. It is okay if I give you a call if I have questions along the way?" Meredith asked.

"You're welcome to anytime. Good luck, and keep me updated on your progress!"

CHAPTER THIRTEEN

FOLLOW YOUR PASSION

While everything she had learned from David Blackford was fresh in her mind, she contacted her friend, Eric Figueroa. She and Eric had met through mutual friends and had known each other for years. They hadn't seen each other in a while, but sending him a Facebook message, she hoped to change that.

Meredith had to admit she was nervous about approaching him. What if he said no? What if he laughed at her idea? Realizing her fears were about the future, she returned to the present. Like David Chametzky had advised in the seminar, she needed to break this down. She could move past this anxiety one minute at a time.

By the time she met Eric at the coffee shop, she had grown legs. She'd taken some time to rehearse her proposal to him, using some of the tips David Blackford had taught her. Her idea was at the conceptualization stage, and this was a time to be creative and collaborate. She truly believed this was an opportunity for both of them. She just hoped Eric agreed.

"Hi, Eric!" she said when he walked in. "It's so good to see you again. You look great!"

"So do you. I like the new hairstyle, Mer," he replied.

"Thanks. I decided to break the mold and try something new," she laughed. "Let's grab a cup of coffee and sit down so we can talk."

After ordering their coffee, they sat at a corner table, one Meredith had personally chosen because it wasn't in the stream of foot traffic. She didn't want there to be any disruptions while she presented her idea. And she wasted no time.

"Eric, first, I want to thank you for sharing your book with me. *The Courageous Cookie* is one of Matthew's favorites. As a matter of fact, I've recorded myself reading it to him, so my mom can play it for him when she has him overnight. It's a bedtime ritual," she said.

"I'm glad to hear it. Writing is my passion—you know that. I'm hoping to turn my passion into my vocation one day," he said.

"Eric, I think I might have a way you can begin to do that, which is why I asked you to meet me today," Meredith replied.

"Now you have my interest. What do you have in mind, Meredith?"

Meredith then presented her idea to him. She told him that she'd been on a journey of professional growth that had put different people in her path and had learned so much, including business principles, keys to success, and how to reinvent herself and overcome fears. In the process, she learned she had to find her purpose and her identity. It was something she couldn't do alone, and everyone she met was put in her path for a reason.

"I've met some truly incredible people! One of the gentlemen's names was also Eric—Eric Power. He works with veterans, helping them get the benefits they deserve. It was Eric Power who inspired me to want to help those who serve our country in some way. I just didn't know how," she explained.

"I applaud that decision, Meredith. But there's more, right?"

"Oh, yes. As fate would have it, the universe kept putting other veterans in my path. Even those who didn't personally serve in the military brought up a common theme—serving others. I've met people with inspiring stories who have served in different branches of the military. Believe me, their service wasn't easy. Some of them were single parents, like me, and they had to leave their kids on the holidays and when they were deployed for extended periods of time. That's where you come in, Eric," Meredith said.

"Go on," he said, waiting.

"I already told you that I read to Matthew every night. A lot of parents do. But think about those parents who are serving our country and can't be home to read to their kids anymore. That's tough on everyone," Meredith said.

"I'm sure it is," he replied.

Taking a deep breath, Meredith got to her point.

"Eric, I want to start a not-for-profit organization to provide servicemembers with services that aren't included in their benefits. For example, childcare for long 36-hour duties and holidays, all paid for through the organization. And meals! So many servicemembers aren't near their families. They don't have the support system many of us have. My friend, Tatjana, told me that she couldn't afford turkey and the fixings on Thanksgiving, and she met a stranger, a veteran, who invited her to his house with other veterans. We could provide them with that meal—and their military family to share it with on holidays like Thanksgiving!"

"We?" Eric countered.

"Well, yes. Let me explain because there's another component to all of this. When they're serving, servicemembers can't read bedtime stories to their kids. They can't sing them a lullaby. What if we gave them the next best thing—a bear or doll that allows them to record those stories and songs to their child?"

"Where do I come in?" Eric asked.

"I don't want the typical kids' fairy tales. I want these to be unique stories with a positive message, like *The Courageous Cookie*. Eric, I want you to write the books that will come with these dolls—books intended just for them. We could sell the books and dolls as part of our fundraising efforts. Eric, I believe you would be a phenomenal partner in this venture and could contribute so much. You're always trying to make a positive impact on others, and you have the business experience to lend, as well," Meredith stated.

"Thank you. I appreciate everything you said. And I do believe your idea has merit. But it would take a lot of work. A not-for-profit organization will require fundraising, volunteers, and marketing. There are legal regulations and financial considerations. We're talking long hours, Meredith. And it might take years before you can implement your full vision," Eric posed.

"I know, but once the idea came to me, it has only grown stronger. You see, Eric, I've grown unhappy with my job, and I thought it was because of low sales and financial instability, but I now know it's not what I want to do for the rest of my life. I want to make a difference and spread a positive message, like you do with your books and stories," Meredith said.

"I can see that this would give me an opportunity to do what I love, which is writing, and making a difference. And my business experience could be a benefit, as well. But a not-for-profit is a business, Mer. It would have to be run like a business, or it could fail, like most businesses do within the first five years," he said.

"I know. Eric, we would need to find someone who can guide us through the process and show us what we need to know about startups and entrepreneurism. We need a business ownership mentor who knows what it takes to be successful," she replied.

"Hmmm, let me think," Eric said, taking a drink of his coffee. "Wait! I do know someone. She has her own business and has started a movement called Take the Plastic Pledge. Perhaps, she would be willing to help."

"What's her name?"

"Lisa Paul Heydet. She owns a company that sells environmentally friendly storage and organization bags. She calls them ZizzyBee Bags. Before we commit to anything, let's talk to her and get some insight into what's involved," he suggested.

"That sounds like a good plan to me. And, Eric, I also don't want you to rush into this, either. I want you to take some time to consider this partnership. We both need to be on board if we're going to make this work," Meredith said.

"I must say it does sound enticing. Let's both give it some thought, and after we talk to Lisa, we'll know what we want to do," he said. "I'll give her a call and see if she's free next weekend."

CHAPTER FOURTEEN

BE A SOLUTION SOLVER, NOT A PROBLEM CREATOR

Lisa agreed to meet the next Saturday morning at her home. It was a beautiful day, and Meredith was excited to meet Lisa and learn about her company.

Eric Figueroa made the introduction.

"Meredith, I want you to meet Lisa Paul Heydet. Lisa, this is my friend, Meredith Grant," he said.

"It's so good to meet you, Lisa. Thank you for taking the time to talk to us on a Saturday. We'll try not to take up too much of your time," Meredith said.

"I'm happy to help in any way I can," Lisa replied.

They sat at a table, and Lisa pulled out a large binder.

"This binder contains some important documents, including my business plan and my company's annual goals," she said. "Before we get started, though, let me tell you about my company. I own a reusable storage bag company. ZizzyBee Bags are see-through, durable, and washable storage bags that replace plastic disposable bags. The focus is on storage and organization, as well as the environment."

"That's why we contacted you, Lisa," Eric said. "You've already launched a business, and we hope you can guide us through the process."

"There are many aspects to consider when launching your own business. In the very beginning, you need to ascertain if your product or service has a market. I encourage you to make sure you do the market research and learn as much as you can about your business and your demographic and who to target."

"Your market research will tell you a lot, but also know that there will be a lot of unknowns. For that reason, you have to be flexible. There are some things you cannot control, so you need to manage what you *can* control," Lisa advised.

"What type of things can we control?" Meredith asked.

"Communication is one. You can control the feedback you'll get from other people. Some of that will be negative. Therefore, it's important to surround yourself with people who support you. If you have to, limit your communication to mentors, consultants, and business colleagues you can trust and who will give you good advice. They should be people outside of your friendship circle. Don't listen to negative opinions, because they will attempt to influence and discourage you," Lisa said.

"Another thing you can control is your knowledge. There are certain things you need to know to successfully run a business, and you might need to take some business courses to bring yourself up to speed. Often, people think they can learn as they go, but trial and error isn't the best approach when it comes to owning a business. As a business owner, you'll find that you are a jack of all trades. But you cannot do it all. Focus on your strengths, and outsource the areas where you are weak or assign them to other people. I highly recommend you have a good bookkeeper, as well as a business coach to consult with, at least in the beginning."

"What were your biggest challenges, Lisa?" Eric asked

"It's easy to become frustrated when something doesn't go as planned," Lisa answered. "Originally, though, I had an issue I didn't foresee with my first manufacturer. I could have given up, but I didn't. I took a step back and did some more research and found a different manufacturer. These types of things will happen. You have to have the perseverance and determination to keep moving forward. If you do believe in your product and have done the research and testing, you will stick to it. I knew people loved my bags because it helped them become organized. That is what kept me going, but I learned early on that sometimes I have to make changes and be adaptable. You might have to add something. For example, my bags were initially intended for toy storage, like Legos. But it grew into something bigger, and the bags have found so many other uses. People love the fact that they reduce plastic waste, and it's grown so much that I started a movement called TakethePlasticPledge.com, which is focused on reducing the plastic waste in our oceans."

"I like that, and it supports ZizzyBee Bags very well," Meredith said.

"Yes, it does. When you have time, I encourage you to visit the website and join the cause," Lisa suggested. "It's my passion. But I've discovered that there will be ups, but there will also be lots of downs. If you have the passion and are adaptable, you can survive. Passion is important, and it is why you do what you do. But it will only get you so far, but remember, this is a business, and emotions need to be set aside. Put yourself in the position of being a customer and take the emotion out of it."

Lisa then opened her binder and turned it around so Eric and Meredith could see the contents.

"This is my business plan, and I cannot stress enough just how important it is for you to have one and stick to it at all times. We'll go through it step by step in a few minutes, but one thing I want you to know is that your business plan isn't just about starting and operating a business—it also needs to address something that some people forget," Lisa said.

"What's that?" Meredith asked.

"You need to address how you will leave the business. You need to include an exit plan in your goals for the foreseeable future. People start businesses all the time, and businesses do fail. An exit plan will address your strategy in the event the business folds or you decide to leave the business," Lisa explained.

They spent the next two hours reviewing ZizzyBee Bags' business plan, while Lisa explained each section.

"The intent of the business plan is to create a plan for success. When you have a well-thought out business plan and you really stick to it, you'll find that you become a solution solver, not a problem creator," Lisa added. "Operating your business according to your plan reminds you that your business is not a hobby. It is something you should take very seriously, and it deserves the opportunity to succeed."

"Well, it looks like we've got a lot of work to do, Eric," Meredith said. "We need to do market research, identify our strengths and weaknesses, create a business plan, find a manufacturer, and ..."

"And you have to name your business, Meredith. Do you have a business name yet?" Lisa asked.

"No, not yet," Meredith replied.

"When you come up with one, you first need to make sure someone else isn't already using it. If they're not, make sure you call a trademark lawyer and get a trademark, so nobody else can use it," Lisa advised.

"That's just the beginning of the many things you need to address when you're starting a business," Lisa added. "There will be other things along the way, I assure you. But like I said earlier, some of those are not foreseeable. They include your business, as well as your family. As a single mom who was starting my own company, I had to set priorities in order to balance my kids, my passion, and my work."

"I have a four-year-old son and can see that I might struggle with that, as well," Meredith interjected. "How did you do it?"

"Let your child be involved in the business. You're setting an example for your son. Use it as an opportunity to teach your child about entrepreneurship. Both of you will learn real life skills you can't learn elsewhere. There will be times when it is hard, but you can do it if you surround yourself with a core group who can help you. This is a good time to connect with other single parents, Meredith, who understand your unique challenges and will lend you the support you need when you need it," Lisa said.

"Talking about my son, I think it's time to pick him up soon. Lisa, thank you so much for taking time out of your busy schedule and away from your family to talk to us," Meredith said.

"Yes, thank you," Eric added. "Lisa, you've been very helpful. I'm sure we are going to have questions as we move forward. Is it okay if we reach out to you from time to time?"

"Absolutely! I want to hear about your progress, and if I can help you find solutions to any problems, I'm happy to do so!" Lisa answered.

CHAPTER FIFTEEN

SERVING OTHERS

Lisa was right—there was a *lot* to do, and Meredith and Eric spent the next 20 months setting up their not-for-profit, Serving Our Soldiers. Meredith created a team, including many of her mentors, to research their demographic and discover their unmet needs and challenges. Eric was busy writing a series of books about courage that would appeal to children. Together, they designed a stuffed bear that they named the SOS Bear, which would record and play back the stories read by their parent who served in the military.

There were times when it was exhausting, especially because Meredith continued to work in the insurance office. Thankfully, the advice of her mentors had gotten her through the lull in sales and she'd been able to boost her sales and, therefore, her commissions. During the night and on the weekends, she worked on the organization at home, and whenever she could, she took Matthew with her to various meetings and fundraisers.

On the day of their opening, Meredith looked back and felt all of the emotions—the excitement, fear, disappointment, and reward. Her mentors had been incredibly unselfish as they shared their knowledge and lent their support, so she made sure they were invited to the ceremony where they announced the opening of the organization and introduced their services to servicemembers and their families.

Nearly six years old now, Matthew had grown to know most of her mentors. On the day of the open house, he had no shortage of friends and people to talk to. As she listened to Eric Power provide a short speech in support of SOS's services, Meredith knew that she had done the right thing for herself and her son. They were now part of an incredible community—a family of people who dedicated their lives to serving others. It was only fitting that she and Eric Figueroa could repay that favor.

Turning around, she realized that she hadn't seen Matthew for several minutes and quickly perused the rooms to find him. She sighed in relief when she saw him sitting next to her partner, Eric, as he read the first book in his series, *The Courageous Cookie.*

Smiling, Meredith realized that none of this would have been possible if it hadn't been for the advice and wisdom of the people around her. Some were with her today, and others had faithfully offered their advice and wisdom whenever she called upon them. People helping people—that was the power of proximity, and it was what their not-for-profit was about.

As Meredith listened to *The Courageous Cookie,* she marveled at the fact it, too, showed that everything you need is no further than the people around you.

THE COURAGEOUS COOKIE

Once upon a time, beyond a mountain climb
There was this place—a place so grand,
a thriving village called Cookieland
Where real life cookies worked & played,
and the tastiest treats there were made.

Happily they lived under skies of blue
as their cookie business grew & grew.
Until a mighty wind blew & blew.
It came to town and crashed right through.

By the morning, it finally passed,
But not before their bridge was thrashed.
All the cookies were left aghast...
"Without our bridge, how will we last?"
With Chocolate Mountain over yonder,
No river crossing left them to wonder:
"How will we get our chocolate chips?
"Any ideas, the mayor asked, any tips?"
He desperately pleaded & pleaded,
"A courageous cookie right now is needed!"

All was silent—not a word nor blip,
Until he spoke up, his name was Chip.
"I'll try my best, I'll try and help."
The crowd began to cheer and yelp.

They made a plan, now there was hope,
He would cross the river with a rope.
They tried all day lasso to a branch,
Just like you'd see at a western ranch.

Finally the rope grabbed on tight
They kept on tightening with all their might.

They jumped for joy and delight,
"Chip would cross at morning light!"

Although the water was cold and fast,
he hoped the rope and his strength would last.
Halfway through they cheered and clapped
Then all of a sudden, the rope just snapped!

"Oh my goodness, there goes Chip!"
Down the river he flopped and flipped.
Before too long, he was washed away
They all were shocked without a word to say.
All of Cookieland's hopes and dreams
With Chip, their friend, went downstream.

They all spread out to look for him but had no luck,
boy this looked grim.
For more than an hour,
he clawed and scratched
Until a hanging vine he finally snatched.

He swung himself up with one hand
and flung himself over to dry land.
The biggest ever relief he sighed;
he finally made it to the other side,
But now lost and far from home,
Chip knew he had a ways to roam.

He hoped the trail he chose was right
For hours and hours he hiked 'til night.
Cold and scared, he found a place to sleep
Under the many stars, he heard no peep.
But before long there were some howls.
The sounds moved closer 'til they were growls.
A pack of wolves snarled and stared
Chip tried his best to not look scared.

Would you please help with me with a good deed?
Getting to Chocolate Mountain is what I need.
Without those chips, we'll soon shut down.
Our families would surely soon leave town.

Off to that mountain with his new friends
On a trail that seemed to have no end
After some advice a snake would lend
They believed they were back on track again.

Chip was startled at the snake's loud hiss.
"Stop," Mr. Snake said, "Listen to this!
"If you need any help—go and see:
The Wise Old Owl who lives in that tree."

The tree was big and looked very old
And the Owl was wise, like they were told.
Mr. Owl said, "Okay, now follow me."
He flapped his wings and began to flee.

In a few short miles, they finally found
That enormous, gigantic chocolate mound.
Chip picked away until he filled his sack
"I now have the chocolate but no way back!"

With a whistle and hoot more birds flew in
And Mr. Wise Old Owl said with a grin,
"Pack as much chocolate as we can,
And let's fly Chip back to Cookieland."

He said thanks to the wolves and the snake
Hopped on the first of many flights he'd take
Back home to one of the sweetest places
Into welcoming arms and thankful faces.

A Courageous Cookie he was, indeed,
Who showed courage in a time of need.
When we take the time to help a friend,
We all live happily ever after ... in the end.

(Copyright ©Eric Figueroa, author)

Reprinted with permission

ABOUT THE AUTHORS

 **Dr. Greg Reid:** Bestselling author, acclaimed speaker, master story-teller, and filmmaker, Greg Reid is a natural entrepreneur known for his giving spirit and a knack for translating complicated situations into simple, digestible concepts. As an action-taking phenomenon, strategy turns into fast and furious results, and relationships are deep and rich in the space he orbits.

Published in over 80 books, 32 bestsellers, 5 motion pictures, and featured in countless magazines, Greg shares that the most valuable lessons we learn are also the easiest ones to apply.

Besides being chosen as a Top 10 Speaker by Forbes/ Inc./Entrepreneur, Greg has been hand selected by The Napoleon Hill Foundation to help carry on the teachings found in the bible of personal achievement, *Think and Grow Rich*. His latest movie, *Wish Man*, features the real life story of Frank Shankwitz (a founder of the Make A Wish Foundation).

www.GregReid.com

 **Bonnie Fallin** is an opportunity expert, multimillionaire business entrepreneur, and the owner of multiple businesses. She is a public speaker, author, mentor, and a real estate investor and stock market investor.

Bonnie opened her first business in 1991, In 1994, she sold it for a nice profit and entered the real estate industry. By 1997, she had bought her first real estate investment property, In 2006, she had the opportunity to invest into several other businesses, making them the largest of their kind in Texas. After investing for another decade, she was blessed to do what she had desired for years, helping others achieve success by recognizing the opportunities around them.

She now has combined her impressive experience in building a multimillion business and coaching into a coaching program, OpportunitySpecs. Bonnie is looking forward to the opportunity to coach and lead you to your greatest dreams by showing you the opportunities surrounding you. To learn more, visit OpportunitySpecs.com.

 **Shannon Parsons** is an empathetic leader whose experience is a unique blend of transformational leadership mixed with a delivery mechanism of heart-centered structure. As a former Transformational Coach & Facilitator, Shannon has partnered with some of the largest organizations in the world as a speaker, facilitator, and trainer to executives, entrepreneurs, and business organizations who need to level up their expertise. Known fondly by senior executives like Greg Reid, founder of Secret Knock, and Scott Duffy, Top Business and Global Business Coach, as "The Secret Weapon," Shannon is often behind the scenes and on the stage as a key emcee and host. Most recently, Shannon launched Secret Knock Women, an event dedicated to focus on true women's empowerment and positive growth. As part of the operational business and brand architect for SideXSide, Shannon is currently leading key initiatives to drive solution-focused groups authorized by the Mastermind Association.

To learn more or contact Shannon, visit shannonparsons.com.

FEATURED AUTHORS

(in order of appearance)

 **Michele Malo** is a best-selling author, speaker, and restoration specialist. She is the Chief Success Officer at Your Business Accelerator, where she identifies, strategizes, and advances businesses by breaking down barriers through personal branding, infrastructure/team development, communication and marketing. Michele pulls from 18 years of Fortune 500 corporate experience as a turn around and restoration specialist within the food service industry. She has advanced knowledge of the manufacturing process, which includes product innovation, financial management, sales and team development, and 8 years of being a successful entrepreneur in the fields of wellness, consulting, and speaking.

As a powerful and polished speaker, Michele inspires audiences with her personal story and proven strategic principles to help guide audiences with The Five Steps to Restoring Your Spark In Business, Health and Relationships. She provides listeners with actionable tools and takeaways based on extensive research and education, delivered with sincerity, compassion and humor. It is time to restore your life's spark, so you can start living life like your hair is on fire. Please visit www.MicheleMalo.com.

Krystylle Richardson is a fun, energetic, no-nonsense, keep it real, warm-hearted soul. Simply put, Krystylle loves seeing people become better versions of themselves mentally, physically, spiritually, financially, emotionally, and more. She is an Interactive Transformational Keynote Speaker, Ambassador of Kindness Minister, Corporate & Personal Mindset & Leadership Coach, and a Business Strategy Mentor. She is ultra-focused on results for the corporate clients and individuals she coaches. She has led and contributed to increased profitability global clients and individuals. She is an ordained Minister and Counselor, has a B.S. in Engineering, and is a Certified Auditor and Six Sigma Green Belt. Her operational excellence and business strategies have been categorized as freakin' brilliant, and her counseling and coaching as sincere and transformational. Her dynamic radio show, Soaring With Eagles, has been heard by thousands throughout almost 40 countries. She has taught and spoken in approx. 25 countries. Krystylle has come to a point where she will not back down from sharing her voice, her triumph over trials (regarding being bullied), her strength, her greatness and helping others do the same.

For more info, go to KrystylleRichardson.com, Instagram at @iamkrystylle, FB @ Krystylle Richardson, join the FB group "Above Your Best Greatness Gathering." Mention this book and get a free gift.

 **David S. Chametzky** is a mentor and coach who has worked internationally and has become a NYS Certified Peer Recovery Advocate, while using various techniques to assist those in finding the right resources for them. David graduated from the University of Maryland with a bachelor's degree in Behavioral Sciences and has enjoyed a successful career in both the corporate and private world for the past 20-plus years. David enjoys sharing his knowledge with those who are passionate about personal and professional development, including business leaders, educators, students, athletes, and law enforcement personnel. He facilitates growth for those who are intent on finding their own P.A.T.H. (Personal Attitudes Toward Happiness) in life. David has worked with individuals and couples, and presented to groups on a number of topics to assist people to move forward toward finding their best self. To contact David, visit DavidChametzky.com or send an email to onthepathny@gmail.com.

 **Johanna Godinez:** An MBA by education and Wellness Coach by trade, Johanna Godinez has always been inspired by the changes we can create for ourselves and others when we become empowered by our capabilities and out internal strength. Johanna received a Marketing degree at NIU and has an MBA at Strayer University, and she knew that her background in business would allow her to build a company

that could help others and change the world. As a lifestyle and wellness educator, KUSI News go-to life coach, Yoga Alliance Continuing Education Provider, Speaker and Human Success Development Coach, the last 10 years have allowed her calling and her passion to impact thousands of individuals nationally and internationally.

In 2011 while doing soul searching, Johanna had a revelation that helped her understand that health is not just your body and lifestyle, it is your finances, your mental attitude, your relationships, your spirituality, and so much more. Through Life and Style Coaches, she is now able to not only assist you in your physical wellness journey, but also allows you to discover the true joy that comes from finding peace inside. As she learned researched the true concerns of the human experience, she discovered that happiness, or lack thereof, depends on the factors that affect overall human health. By building a life map and taking into account the 8 factors of overall human health, she allows you the ability to discover how your situation is related to your state of mind and how you can create the changes necessary to start driving the direction of your life. The aim is to offer you awareness of your current situations and assist you in altering your habits and implementing solutions to help you obtain the life you have always dreamed of.

To learn more about Johanna, please visit https://lifeandstylecoaches.com.

 **Eric Louis Power** served honorably in the United States Navy from the years 2002 to 2012, in which time, Eric reached the rank of Petty Officer First Class. Eric served in Operation Iraqi Freedom, Operation Enduring Freedom, and Operation Southern Watch and has a total of seven deployments, with 3.5 years in active combat zones.

Since separating from the service, Eric began helping other Veterans with their VA Disability Claim after securing his 100% Permanent and Total in 2012. A merchant at heart, Eric created Veterans Disability Help, LLC while pursuing his first business degree. Since then, Eric has achieved his MBA and currently dedicates himself full time as Chief Executive Officer of Veterans Disability Help, LLC.

Eric has a passion for helping, not only his brothers and sisters in arms. He personally founded the non-profit "For Veterans By Veterans," which is focused on helping homeless veterans. He also is a standing board member for the nonprofit "Brighter Future," a registered 501©3.

Eric has streamlined the system to maximize the efforts put forth by the Veterans in regard to their Disability Compensation.

Eric is currently married to his wife, Chikako Suzuki – Power, with two beautiful girls, Maya Lynn Power and Mia Lynn Power.

For more information, visit veterandisabilityhelp.com.

 **Daniel Mangena:** After receiving a late diagnosis of Asperger's and experiencing what can only be described as life-shattering trauma at the age of just 20, Daniel Mangena spent the next seven years struggling to keep these revelations and events from spilling into every area of his life. As a result of his struggles, Daniel built a simple, four-step system called the Beyond Intention Paradigm.

Initially built as a lifeline grappling with suicidal thoughts, Beyond Intention was born, transforming Daniel's life from misery to celebration. Through his own struggles, Daniel found a path to lasting joy and purpose and he wants nothing more than to share the tools that saved his life.

Through motivational speech, Daniel shares his vision of empowerment and joy, as well as via books he has authored, his "Do it With Dan" podcast series (which is available on all major platforms), frequent blogging, articles, and a series of worldwide workshops. Daniel also offers coaching and consultations in groups and in one-on-one sessions. Each of these sessions honors his mission and helps his clients find meaning and joy in their lives. He is also an outspoken promoter of entrepreneurial philanthropy, as well as an ambassador for the Mangena Foundation (in addition to working with several charities across the globe).

To contact Daniel, go to www.dreamwithdan.com. He can also be found on most major social media platforms with the handle @dreamerCEO.

Tatjana Omanović was born in Hamburg, Germany. She grew up in Serbia while it was still part of the Socialist Federative Republic of Yugoslavia. She became intimately familiar with stress and deprivation at an early age, and sought a way to a better life. She heard about a place called America... Overcoming repeated rejections, she immigrated to America at age 16, enlisted in the Marine Corps at age 20, and retired a Gunnery Sergeant after 20 years of service to her adopted home. She settled down in Carlsbad, CA to raise four sons and inspire greatness in others.

Tatjana's continuing education is focused on cognitive neuroscience, psychology, and the human mind. Her greatest joys are found in learning, teaching, and inspiring others to grow! As a seasoned leader and gifted "seer," Tatjana fuses her experience with her intuition to deliver breakthroughs and continued motivation for individuals and teams. As the Co-Founder of The Best You Legacy Club in Carlsbad, CA, Tatjana is committed to both community and collaboration! Tatjana's mission is to provide personal and professional wellness for veterans and civilians alike! Please contact Tatjana at tatjana.omanovic@gmail.com.

Krysten Maracle's Federal career at Naval Information Warfare Center Pacific as a civilian for the Department of the Navy has spanned over 3 decades. Her technical expertise is in Communication Systems and Cyber-security. Before retiring in 2019, Krysten worked extensively with Joint Services (Navy, Army, Air Force and Marines) in various roles.

As a founding member of the Mastermind Association, as well as a "Certified Mastermind Leader" from Dr. Greg Reid, Krysten became the Chief Executive Officer (CEO) of Maracle Mastermind, INC. in 2019 in order to pursue her passions in life by helping and giving to others. Maracle Mastermind organizes events regularly throughout the year for the purpose of solving challenges (i.e., interviewing various doctors, nurses, and nutritionalists regarding COVID-19), exploring new opportunities, and helping others do the same.

Krysten has donated tens of thousands of dollars to Wounded Warriors and is currently working with others to create a two-day Veterans' Program called "Creating Freedom for Your Future." Determined to help abused and/or underprivileged men, women, and children, she volunteers with others to provide support, food, toys in an "Everything Drive" in Tijuana, Mexico. Contact Krysten at maracle.travel@gmail.com and Instagram and Facebook "Krysten Maracle."

Krysten is most proud of her two young adult, self-reliant and self-sufficient children. Both Kaitlyn and Nathan graduated from Cal Poly San Luis Obispo (SLO) with degrees in Agriculture Business and Civil Engineering respectively.

David Blackford: Founder at Blacklock Designs, David Blackford is the creator and founder of Ancherz® and the co-founder and principal at A-Leg-UP®. "I find passion in the process of creation, and I am forever grateful for the opportunities to give birth to a new concept or idea."

David Blackford is a native Californian. In 1987, the Navy brought him to San Diego, where he has lived for more than 30 years. In 2011, his father asked him for help in the building of a business around an invention he created, called A-Leg-UP®. Since then, he has created the brand called Ancherz and has formed a company (Blacklock Designs) to umbrella these products and others yet to be born. Currently, he is working with Launch Factory, a company looking to form a joint venture for future product creation.

Business aside, David loves spending time with his family and friends. He enjoys golfing and looks for ways to help or volunteer. He has built homes in Mexico, been on mission trips to Vietnam, and has volunteered for the PGA for the past 10 years. In 2020, he was fortunate enough to walk with Phil Mickelson, Jordan Spieth, and Tiger Woods.

David believes we are placed on this planet to serve and be happy. He has found that the more you do for others, the more you receive in return. He encourages other to share their gifts.

If you have a thought and or an idea and are not sure what to do with it, please send an email to David at askdave@blacklockdesigns.com.

Eric Figueroa is a published author and poet. He has penned hundreds of poems, as well as five children's stories, including "The Courageous Cookie," "The Bully and The Bullfrog," "Sidney The Squirrel," "Mean Mr. Green," and "Our Magic Bakery." Eric Figueroa has lived in southern California his entire life. This husband, father and grandfather focuses on weaving positive messages within his writing, knowing that words are powerful and can make a difference in our lives.

You can contact Eric Figueroa by sending an email to him at ericfig2000@yahoo.com.

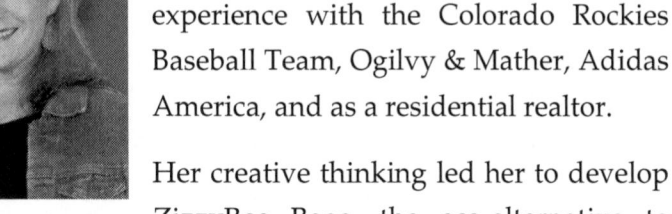

Lisa Paul Heydet graduated from the University of San Diego and has acquired extensive marketing and advertising experience with the Colorado Rockies Baseball Team, Ogilvy & Mather, Adidas America, and as a residential realtor.

Her creative thinking led her to develop ZizzyBee Bags, the eco-alternative to conventional single-use, plastic bags. ZizzyBee bags are reusable, washable, see-through, last forever, have a convenient zipper, and also have an easy hang or hold loop. A 3-pack of ZizzyBee Bags saves 1000+ single use plastic bags a year per household. Lisa also launched a movement called Take the Plastic Pledge and has partnered with dozens of eco brands to offer a one-stop shop of plastic alternative or recycled plastic products. Ten percent of all Swap Shop sales are donated to The Ocean Clean Up Project with a goal to raise one million dollars and get one million pledgers.

If you would like to learn more about Lisa and ZizzyBee Bags, visit www.zizzybeebags.com and www.taketheplasticpledge.com.